Understanding Specific Learning Difficulties

Margot Prior

*Departments of Psychology, University of
Melbourne and LaTrobe University, and The
Royal Children's Hospital, Melbourne, Australia*

Psychology Press
An imprint of Erlbaum (UK) Taylor & Francis

Psychology Press, Publishers
27 Church Road
Hove
East Sussex, BN3 2FA
UK

British Library Cataloguing in Publication Data

A catalogue record for this book is available from the British Library

ISBN 0-86377-712-0 (hbk)
ISBN 0-86377-713-9 (pbk)

Cover design by Joyce Chester
Printed and bound in the United Kingdom by Biddles Ltd., UK

Contents

Acknowledgements

Many people have contributed to the development of this book, not least my graduate psychology students at LaTrobe University, during many years of teaching, collaborative research, and clinical work. Together we have learned much about children who are struggling at school.

Diana Smart and Ric Pawsey read and commented on early drafts of the book, and their reactions provided valued contributions. I thank Lynne Roberts, Mary Iliadis, and Katy Cole for their help with the manuscript and reference preparation.

CHAPTER ONE

Introduction: Specific learning difficulties defined

At least one in every ten children of school age will have difficulties with one or more areas of the school curriculum, most commonly reading and spelling. A proportion will overcome early difficulties, but for the majority, learning difficulties are likely to persist and to have deleterious consequences on their later careers. Fewer than one in ten, however, will actually be identified as needing help, and be able to receive a formal diagnosis of "Specific Learning Difficulties". But, whether officially diagnosed with a disability or not, a disturbing number of children are having a very discouraging and unhappy time in the classroom. Learning difficulties are a widespread and significant individual and social problem.

HISTORY OF THE CONCEPT OF LEARNING DIFFICULTIES

From an historic point of view, the intensive study of learning difficulties began to develop around the time of the Second World War. At that time, researchers began to systematically study soldiers with missile injuries that had affected their brain functioning. Some of the consequences of the damage to the brain involved loss of particular cognitive abilities including difficulties with specific aspects of memory and learning, and sometimes, reading, writing, and calculating abilities. Since that time, there have been rapidly accumulating data exploring links between damage to particular areas of the brain and ensuing or "acquired" cognitive disorders.

The early findings of this research showing that individuals could lose the ability to read after accidental brain trauma, led people to the inference that children with developmental or "congenital" specific learning and behaviour difficulties might have some form of brain damage which "caused" their problems, even if the damage was not apparent to the observer, or was of a very subtle kind. This "biological" or neurological approach to interpreting childhood learning difficulties failed to take into account the enormous complexity of the relationships between brain and behaviour, and our relative ignorance of the early stages of the development of reading and writing skills. But it was productive in leading to the growth of more systematic attempts to understand the nature and origins of childhood learning difficulties (see Farnham-Diggory, 1978, for a brief review of early work).

Even earlier though, Hinshelwood (1895) and Orton (1925) had developed speculative neurological theories regarding specific problems with reading and suggested that there were particular problems with the brains of children who could not read. Their observations and descriptions of individual cases, and their beliefs about the origins of the observed problems have over the years been shown to be far too simplistic, in light of more advanced knowledge of brain function as well as further understanding of the developmental aspects of learning to read. Nevertheless they have been influential as springboards for theories that have been developed and elaborated since early this century. Contemporary theories relating brain systems to aspects of learning will be reviewed in more detail in Chapters 2 and 5.

WHAT DO WE MEAN BY SPECIFIC LEARNING DIFFICULTIES?

There are many and various definitions of the term "specific learning difficulties". The parent, teacher, or professional is likely to be somewhat confused by the variety of terms used. Concepts and labels which abound in this field cover problems such as hyperactivity and attention disorders, language delay and deficits, including developmental dysphasia; mild intellectual disability, "clumsy children"; "minimal brain dysfunction"; perceptual problems, social and emotional problems; slow learner, children in special education,—the list could go on. How is the parent, teacher, or health professional to find a way through the maze of terminology that permeates the research literature as well as attitudes in health and educational settings where learning-disabled children are seen? Some of these terms will be discussed in the following chapters of this book in the context of particular views of learning difficulties. For example, the relevance of language delay and difficulties will be covered in the chapter on neuropsychology, and hyperactivity and socio-emotional problems in the chapter on the association between learning difficulties and behaviour disorders.

The study of specific learning difficulties is also a field where many myths have been created over the years. A vast amount of research continues to accumulate and it often seems that the grounds of our understanding shift continuously, with new trends and fashions coming along in a constant parade of changing approaches to the problems. At its most general level, learning difficulty means failure to learn basic academic skills so that temporary, or more likely, enduring disabilities are the consequence. In some countries, children with intellectual handicaps, i.e. with intelligence below the normal range, are called "learning-disabled", perhaps in an attempt to make the term intellectual disability a little less stigmatising. Teachers and parents sometimes prefer to refer to their intellectually disabled child as having a learning disability. Although this is undoubtedly a true description, as intellectually disabled children are slower to learn than normal, these children are in a different category and are not the focus here.

This book is concerned with "specific learning difficulties" (hereafter abbreviated as SLD); that is, problems in learning that cannot be easily explained by lack of intellectual ability or by deficient schooling. The term would of course have no meaning in a country where children did not receive a formal education, as their academic achievement would not be an issue. It is a product mainly of the Western world where enormous value is placed on doing well at school, and where unpredictable and unexplained failure is of great concern to the child and his or her family and teachers.

Children with SLD arising early in development have difficulty learning in one or more areas for somewhat mysterious or poorly understood reasons. The term is not applied to children whose educational history has been one of deprivation and disruption because the problem could be lack of opportunity rather than a function of problems within the child. Poor-quality education can handicap basic literacy and numeracy skills but is more likely to affect learning success generally rather than striking specific areas. Some definitions exclude children with known physical or organic handicaps even though they may have difficulties with learning. However it is perfectly possible to have an organic condition (such as cerebral palsy) and be SLD or not SLD.

A definition based on the current literature and which is generally acceptable is that the child with SLD should have:

> an IQ score greater than 80, and deficits in at least one area of academic achievement (reading, spelling, mathematics), associated with specific cognitive impairments (such as short term memory problems, poor auditory discrimination ability, visuo-perceptual problems, and the like).

This definition brings in the notion of impairments in brain processes which are the underpinnings (or possibly the explanations) of the SLD. These will be discussed in Chapter 5. However, it should be noted that the quantity and quality of evidence for neurological abnormalities in SLD children is poor, and any connection between brain abnormalities and learning difficulties is obscure in most cases. Hence it may be argued that the latter part of this definition is speculative.

READING DISABILITY

It needs to be noted at the outset that there has been far more attention paid to children with reading disability than with any other learning problems, both in research studies and in educational settings. Therefore we are much further advanced in our understanding of how children learn to read and why some of them fail, by comparison with other LDs such as those involving mathematics. Reading problems have been emphasised, not only because they are such a handicap in industrialised societies, but also because they are usually just the more prominent or easily recognised aspect of LDs which exist across the three Rs (Reading, Riting, and Rithmetic).

In regard to reading disability (hereafter called RD) there are a number of terms used, such as dyslexia, specific reading retardation, backward readers, disabled readers etc., (Rutter & Yule 1975), which often confuse people and which need clarification.

What is dyslexia?

Dyslexia is a medically oriented term which simply means abnormal reading. The definition of dyslexia promulgated by the World Federation of Neurology is: a disorder manifested by difficulty in learning to read despite conventional instruction, adequate intelligence, and socio-cultural opportunity. It is dependent on fundamental cognitive disabilities which are frequently of constitutional origin. This is a diagnosis using exclusionary criteria, i.e. dyslexia is what you have left when all possible causes have been eliminated. This is a most unsatisfactory term, because it leaves most of the problem unexplained. However the label has a certain mystique about it which makes it appealing to researchers seeking for definable syndromes with measurable symptoms and identifiable (generally biological) causes. Parents and teachers also sometimes like this term because it suggests that the problem might be a medical one which therefore could have a medical (biological) explanation and cure. Of course this is not the case at all, as there is no prescription or medical-type cure for dyslexia.

Dyslexia in childhood or "developmental dyslexia" is seen as a congenital form of "alexia" or "dyslexia" which has been found in adults who have *lost* the ability to read as a result of brain damage, following trauma such as stroke, tumour, accidental head injury, brain disease, etc., usually when such injury is associated with parts of the left or language side of the brain. In the early years of the study of RD it was assumed that children failing to learn to read must have some form of left brain damage where the centres associated with the ability to read were damaged or malfunctioning in some way from birth. In recent years there have been some studies comparing the reading of acquired, or adult, cases and developmental cases of "dyslexia" which have shown some similarities in the kinds of errors they make (see Snowling, 1987, for discussion of "varieties" of developmental dyslexia). However the extent to which one can compare children who are in the process of learning to read, with adults whose early learning history is not always clear and who, in any case, have usually had years of experience with reading before the occurrence of their trauma, is very limited.

It can be argued that there is nothing specific about dyslexic children as distinct from RD children given a variety of other labels. "Specific reading retarded children" as categorised by Rutter and Yule (1975), and McGee et al. (1986) is another label given to children who are average or above in intelligence but who are 18 months or more behind in reading, i.e. this delay is unexpected taking into account their IQ level. One of the many problems is that researchers differ in how far "behind" they expect a child to be before he or she attracts a particular label. This can vary from 12 months to 2 or 3 years, or one or more grades.

"Backward reader" is a term that has been used for children who are behind in reading achievement but whose intelligence is below normal, and hence their delay may not be unexpected given their intellectual delay. However, many researchers have found that categorisation of such children into specific reading retarded or backward is rather unstable, as they may change categories as they develop. Specific retarded readers may turn into backward readers if their reading problems handicap their learning and lead to a drop in measured IQ such that they drift below the normal range. As we are concerned with *developmental* problems, it is wise to remember that change is inevitable; nothing is fixed about SLDs, either in their specific nature or in their course over time. There do not appear to be differences in longer term outcome for specific versus backward readers; initial severity of RD is the major predictive factor.

Shaywitz et al. (1992) have reported longitudinal data which shows that dyslexia, or RD, whichever the problem is called, is part of a continuum, or varies by degree just as normal reading skills do; it is not an all or none category of disability.

Furthermore, there is no evidence that children diagnosed as dyslexic, or specific reading retarded, differ at all from children with (non categorised) reading problems who have one of the disadvantages mentioned in the definition of dyslexia. For example, many RD children also have behavioural or emotional disturbance but their reading problems are exactly the same in nature as those in children with no behavioural disorder. It has not been possible, either, to find any specific cognitive or neurological differences between dyslexic children and those called poor readers, or reading disabled, or whatever label, provided they are within the normal IQ range. Labels therefore can be very confusing and are probably not useful unless they lead to the provision of special resources for the child. They then have functional rather than explanatory significance.

INTELLIGENCE AND ITS RELATIONSHIP TO SLD

A part of the arguments regarding RD is connected to the fact that SLD children are by definition assumed to be in the normal range of intelligence, and therefore they would be expected to be able to read, spell, and calculate. The condition is surprising or unexpected according to this theory. But the relationship between general intelligence and all kinds of other abilities including reading skill is a far from perfect one, so that one cannot assume that normal intelligence is either *necessary* or *sufficient* for normal reading.

This is a controversial issue which has important implications for how SLDs are defined. The use of discrepancy scores, that is a difference or discrepancy between the actual level of reading of the child and that which would be expected according to his or her intellectual capacity, (implying that average IQ should go along with average reading ability for example), has been criticised on many grounds, with no consensus being reached on how to deal with the problem.

One criticism is that failure to learn to read adequately may limit the opportunities for children to acquire the kinds of knowledge that are tested in standard intelligence tests. So estimated IQ, especially in the verbal knowledge area, may be inaccurate, and it is this aspect of intelligence that is most clearly related to RD. Indeed some researchers have shown a decline in IQ over time in children who fail to learn to read. This may not mean that they are becoming less intelligent but just that they are not gathering some of the information needed to help children to do well on modern intelligence tests, many of which rely on acquired verbal learning or academic skills. Testing with measures of "fluid intelligence" or hard-wired mechanical knowledge, which is thought to be biologically based and less dependent on acquired learning, may show RD children to have few difficulties. These kinds of intelligence factors include sensory processing, visual or motor memory, discrimination, categorisation and coordination abilities such as discriminating between geometric forms, or finding strategies to solve practical problems. It is often found that SLD children do well on these kinds of tests and poorly on tests of verbally based acquired knowledge, which might be called the "software" of the brain. Estimates of IQ for SLD children may be subject to bias and unreliability as a *result* of their LDs.

Another criticism is that the relationship between intelligence and reading ability, although strong, is a far from exact one with correlations approximating .7. This leaves a great deal of the variance in reading ability unexplained by intellectual abilities. In other words one should not expect parallel levels of IQ and reading skill because they are imperfectly correlated, thus undermining a major definitional criterion for dyslexia. Siegel (1989) has argued cogently that we do not need IQ test scores in defining learning difficulties because they do not predict the specific cognitive functions central to reading, spelling, and language tasks. Nevertheless there is ongoing debate about "specific" versus "backward" RD definitions with different conclusions emerging from different samples, with different IQ tests, and with varying methods of defining RD. As Snowling (1991, p. 52) notes, "intelligence tests are blunt instruments" and limited in their ability to differentiate cognitive problems relevant to reading skill. It should hardly surprise us that IQ measures are not adequate in distinguishing between groups of individuals with LDs; IQ and "disability" definitions lack precision.

In the field of reading problems, then, there is a plethora of terms which are unhelpful in distinguishing types of difficulties, and using the term "dyslexia" does nothing to sort out the confusion. The precise relationship with levels of intelligence is hard to determine because there are many kinds of intelligences or abilities and not all of them correlate well with academic learning ability.

Other research has shown that there are no differences between SLD children with and without sensory, or IQ deficits, in the ways that they read, nor in the kinds of reading impairments they show, nor on a variety of language, perceptual, and memory tasks. In a 1994 review, Stanovich argued that the reading–IQ discrepancy formula does not identify groups of RD children who differ in significant ways that would validate the conventional differentiation. He suggests that a more productive way of conceptualising RD may be as the mild end of a continuum of developmental language disorder. This way of thinking about reading problems suggests that amongst young children there is a continuum of ability or disability in language capacities.

Children with "developmental language disorder" are handicapped in comprehending language from early in life and have difficulties acquiring a normal level of expressive language, most commonly for unknown reasons. These language handicaps will carry over into the learning of reading skills because the basic building blocks for the print to word translation process are impaired. Children with milder levels of language disorder may also be at risk for reading and spelling difficulties.

However this theory is not an easy one to accept because some children with reading difficulties apparently have perfectly normal language development, and not all children with a developmental language disorder fail to become proficient readers. Furthermore, the incidence of RD is much higher than the incidence of language disorder. Language proficiency is a major component of IQ measures, hence the relationships identified between language disorder and RD may be connected in a complex way via the influence of other aspects of verbal intelligence.

Debates in the field about all of these complex issues will no doubt persist, and identification of SLD children will continue to be based to some extent on subjective criteria and beliefs about whether discrepancy formulae are centrally important or not.

But, to reiterate, this book is concerned with children whose intelligence is in the normal range but who have notable and specific difficulty with reading, writing, and mathematics for no clearly identified reason. Their academic skills are "out of step" with their general ability.

SINGLE OR MULTIPLE SYNDROMES?

Reading, spelling, and numeracy skills are basic to school achievement. SLD children may show problems in all three areas or only one or two. Reading and spelling are closely associated skills and it is rare to find reading-disabled children who are not even more handicapped in spelling. Most children are likely to be behind in all three areas, although there are occasional reports of sub-groups showing rather more of one or the other deficit.

In practice, children who cannot read adequately will have difficulty with spelling because of their deficient store of word-specific knowledge. And they may do poorly at mathematics, if only because they have trouble reading and understanding symbols.

Because of the demonstrated close (albeit not perfect) relationship between reading and spelling problems, the term RD will be used in the discussion of literacy problems, and mathematics disorder will be treated separately in Chapter 3, where the term SMD (specific maths disorder) will be used.

WHAT PROPORTION OF SCHOOL CHILDREN ARE LD?

The true prevalence of SLD is almost impossible to ascertain because different studies use different criteria for identifying SLD children. For example it is possible to use specified distances on the normal curve of abilities to categorise RD children by saying that if they are more than

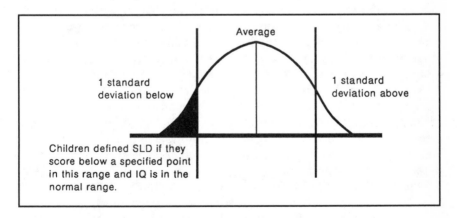

FIG. 1.1. Using the normal distribution curve of abilities to define SLD.

one standard deviation below average (and their IQ is in the normal range), they have significant reading problems.

It is also possible to use a category such as more than 18 months behind the level expected for the child's age, or a reading level more than a certain number of grades below the school grade the child is actually in. It is easy to see how this will produce different estimates of prevalence.

If one uses the criterion of more than one standard deviation below average on reading, spelling, or maths tests, then about 15% of children will be RD or MD. If one takes the more severe end, e.g. one and a half standard deviations, then about 10% of children will be so designated. In whatever way it is calculated, the fact is that a significant number of children suffer from SLDs. At least one or two in every classroom is a fair estimate. Epidemiological studies in Britain indicated that 11% of boys and 6% of girls in an Isle of Wight sample, and 22% of boys and 15% of girls in a London sample were reading at a "low" level (Berger, Yule, & Rutter, 1975).

Because of the relative lack of attention paid to numeracy or mathematics disorders, it is not possible to estimate prevalence, but it is possible that these problems are even more common than RDs. The figure of 6% has been quoted in some studies (e.g. Shalev, Auerbach, & Gross-Tur, 1995), but to what extent this is based on children with specific MD as a single disorder, versus one in combination with literacy problems, and whether it is confined to those whose IQ is in the normal range, is uncertain.

SEX DIFFERENCES IN SLD

It is generally accepted that boys are at higher risk for a whole range of developmental problems in the early years of life. More infant boys die, more boys have developmental disorders such as childhood autism and language disorders, and boys are developmentally somewhat less mature than girls in the first few years, especially in language and social development, (although they have generally "caught up" by the end of primary school). With regard to SLDs, especially those with associated problems such as neurological dysfunction, language delay, and behaviour disorders, boys clearly outnumber girls. The ratio of difference varies with the particular problem but it is particularly marked in the "externalising" or disruptive behaviour disorders where boys may outnumber girls by as much as 10 to 1, and at the very least by 4 to 1. Disruptive behaviour disorders are particularly associated with reading problems. Boys outnumber girls in populations with early language delay or speech problems, which are also central to the development of reading skills. Such male/female differences have led some researchers to postulate sex-linked mechanisms of inheritance of problems, although so far there is minimal evidence to support such theories.

Boys are much more numerous in clinical samples, i.e. children referred for professional help, and it is these samples that provide the bulk of the research data, and upon which the belief in the predominance of boys with SLDs is based. However, it is possible that there could be just as many girls with SLDs, but because they generally do not disrupt the class and cause as many interpersonal, interactional difficulties at school, they may not be referred for help as often. Data from a number of population studies have suggested that girls with SLDs are under-reported by teachers, and they may be as numerous as boys by the middle years of primary school (Prior, Sanson, Smart, & Oberklaid, 1995; Shaywitz, Shaywitz, Fletcher, & Escobar, 1990). Vogel (1990) has argued that girls must be much more learning handicapped, and/or have associated intellectual disability before they receive adequate attention. Although the predominance of boys in referred or clinically defined RD groups is well documented, and they are also more numerous amongst children with difficulties across the three areas of reading, spelling, and maths, there is insufficient study of *specific* spelling and mathematical difficulties to allow estimates of whether boys are also more numerous in these groups. In terms of rates of progress in reading, and of recovery from RD there appear to be no gender differences (Maughan, Hagell, Rutter, & Yule 1994)

It is possible that gender differences in SLD may also be associated with cultural and educational influences. For example, most schools in Western societies tend to have women teaching the kindergarten and lower primary grades. But in Germany where young children are taught to read in the early years by male teachers, it is claimed that reading problems are not more common amongst boys, suggesting a strong modelling effect in these critical early stages of learning.

In a large study of reading achievement in four English speaking nations, across Grades 2, 4, and 6, Johnson (1974) found few gender differences, but those that did exist varied from country to country. In England and Nigeria, boys out performed girls, whereas in Canada and the US girls scored higher than boys. These latter countries also had predominantly female teachers who believed that girls were better readers. Although this was not a study of SLD children, it does suggest that caution is needed in speculating about the biological influences on learning deficits which are often predicated on the belief that this is a mostly male disorder. It is necessary to take into account the range of cultural effects that can make a major difference to the academic outcome of these children. Reading may be much more valued as a skill for girls, whereas boys are urged to get out and be active and this behaviour is modelled by their fathers. Alternatively, boys who show problems may be more readily referred for help because their academic and occupational outcome is seen to be more important than that of girls.

Because so much of the research into SLD has concentrated on the problems of boys, we still have much to learn about the characteristics of SLD girls. Recent studies in the US and in Australia (Prior et al, 1995), have shown that when children are identified as RD by *research criteria* (i.e. according to scores on a reading test administered to a whole sample of the population such as all Grade 2 children in a certain area), there are almost as many girls as boys who are doing poorly. When RD children are identified by the teacher there are many more boys, probably because teachers have been concerned by their behaviour problems as well as their SLDs.

Aaron (1982) reported that the incidence of RD is lowest for Japanese children (who have different writing systems, one logographic or picture symbol based, the other phoneme and syllable based as in English, with the final printed language being a combination of picture and letter symbols), and amongst the highest for English, with other languages falling in between. Five percent is reported for Germany and ten percent for France, but there may well be unknown ascertainment biases as well as some influence of language type. For example, some languages such as Spanish are fully phonetic (all words can be sounded out), whereas some like English are very irregular and unpredictable and may make reading more difficult.

A comparison of Japanese, Chinese, and English Grade 5 children carried out by Stevenson and colleagues in 1982 showed that similar proportions of children from each country showed reading disability, thus arguing against strongly differential influences of language or "orthography" in reading skill. So there are still many uncertainties in this particular debate.

Age of school entry, testing methods used, favoured teaching strategies, and many other variables may affect estimates of SLDs in various countries.

PROPOSED CAUSES

A variety of hypotheses have been proposed to explain SLDs, from intra-uterine damage, to specific brain lesions, to parental neglect. There is some evidence of a genetic component, as RD, at least, often affects more than one family member. An estimate of the concordance rate for RD in identical twins is 71%, compared with 49% in non-identical twins. Family studies suggest that at least one third of RD children have a parent or sibling with a reading problem, compared with around 9% in parents and siblings of non RD children. However the mechanism of inheritance remains speculative. Twin studies have also been used to explore such mechanisms, and recent more sophisticated research which has focused on particular components of reading and spelling skills rather than "literacy" in general, has suggested that it might be one particular aspect of RD that has high heritability—phonological coding capacities (Olson et al., 1989; Stevenson 1991). Perhaps related to this finding is that of Stevenson, Graham, Fredman, and McLoughlin (1987) who, in addition to confirming high heritability for phonological coding, reported that heritability for spelling (which is believed to be more phonologically based) was much higher than that for reading. However these latter findings pertain to a population of 13-year-old twins whose reading problems may have improved while, as is so often the case with RD children, their spelling remains notably impaired. But this kind of detailed genetic research, which looks at component skills in reading and spelling, is valuable in furthering our understanding of underlying mechanisms in SLDs.

In the field of reading problems in particular, there have been numerous theories regarding particular sites of the brain that may be damaged or dysfunctional. Many have suggested that the left or language dominant hemisphere must be abnormal in some way as it is this hemisphere of the brain that is predominant in reading. Studies of adults with left brain damage who have lost the ability to read, underpin these theories. But it is possible to have right-sided brain damage and to acquire SLDs as a consequence, and many left brain damaged people can read normally. Moreover, for children whose brains are still developing and for whom functions are presumed to be less "fixed" or more plastic, and in whom there are no signs of neurological damage, the arguments are tenuous. They will be reviewed in more detail in Chapter 5.

The frankest answer to the question of causation is that we do not know what makes a child develop SLDs. It is possible that they come from a variety of causes; for some children there is a high degree of genetic influence, for some there may be brain dysfunction, for others it is to do with family and social factors and strong disinclination for reading which leads to more and more avoidance. For others it may be to do with early behavioural problems such as "Attention Deficit Hyperactivity Disorder" which interferes with early learning and so sets the child on a course of failure and avoidance. In many cases there will be not one but a variety of interacting influences that lead to SLDs. In the individual case, only careful developmental, clinical, behavioural, educational, and neuropsychological assessment will help in understanding the nature of the problems for that child and why he or she might be SLD.

There are several levels at which one may consider causes. The most basic biological level encompasses hypotheses about genetic influences, or specific brain dysfunction, or damage implicating the left or language side of the brain; or there may be developmental abnormalities in the brain maturation process which may put a child at risk for SLD. To investigate problems at this level we need exploration of the brains of SLD children which is not possible except in highly unusual circumstances. Hence we must rely on theories based on information collected from analyses of brain-damaged adults or sometimes from experimental work with normal populations.

At a behavioural or process level of explanation, there are hypotheses such as faulty eye movements, perceptual difficulties, short-term memory deficits, etc. These hypotheses will be taken up in the context of Chapter 5 which outlines neuropsychological approaches, but at this point it can be claimed that neither perceptual problems, nor eye-movement defects cause reading and spelling problems, even though it is possible to find RD children who show some non-specific difficulties with perceptual tasks. Short-term auditory memory problems are associated with RD although they are not always present in children with such problems, and are sometimes present in children who read perfectly well. This is another popular process-level explanation.

The search for explanations and causes continues to be pursued vigorously but it seems unlikely that any clear and unequivocal answer will be found. The cognitive processing involved in reading, writing, and mathematics is immensely complex; there are enormous individual differences in cognitive skills; and any human behaviour is determined by such a multitude of influences that it is not realistic to expect single simple explanations when things go wrong.

At a level that actually mimics the act of reading, are recent attempts at computer modelling of information processing, including reading. This experimental work may provide us with further insights into how reading difficulties can occur at a cognitive/linguistic processing level, (Coltheart, Curtis, Atkins, & Haller 1993) and hopefully will develop further in modelling the development of learning difficulties (Share, 1995) and how to remedy them.

HOW ARE SLD CHILDREN DIAGNOSED?

Parents of children who are showing little interest, or skill, in reading or writing after the first year or two at school are likely to feel some concern. If they share these concerns with the teacher it is not uncommon for them to be told not to worry because the child will soon catch up; or if there is a problem the child will "grow out of it". However if problems persist and the child is not finding school a rewarding experience, is losing confidence and self esteem, and strenuously avoiding reading and writing as much as possible, parents are likely to become seriously worried and to look for reasons why their child is not making normal progress.

Most teachers in primary school classrooms know who are the children who are failing to keep pace with the rest of the class. In the first couple of years at school, this may be glossed over because children mature at varying rates and some are slower to catch on to the three Rs than others. But by Grade 2, or about 7 years of age, children who are not reading at an age/grade-appropriate level are likely to attract concern. This will be particularly so if they are also showing behavioural problems such as inability to concentrate, to sit still, to organise their work and to finish it without supervision; or if they are disruptive, aggressive, and will not follow class rules and regulations. The majority of children with this combination of problems are boys. Teachers may not be so sensitive in identifying girls who are failing, especially if they do not cause any trouble in the classroom and they are cooperative and pleasant. Hence many LD girls may be missed.

Neither parents nor teachers are always able to judge accurately who is behind because they are below normal intellectual capacity (backward or slow learners), and who is specifically LD. For such a "differential diagnosis", specialised assessment is necessary. This will usually involve a paediatric examination to assess developmental history, neurological integrity, and health problems; psychometric testing to assess intellectual and academic strengths and weaknesses; and behavioural or clinical assessment to help in understanding the psychological characteristics of the child which may be contributing to his or her problems. Analysis of the child's home, school, and community environment is also important. Sometimes testing of vision and hearing will also be required.

For most SLD children there are few or only minor neuro-developmental or physical problems, although there are some associations with medical conditions which can occur with some frequency. Perhaps the most prominent of these is a history of otitis media, or recurrent ear infection. This can give the child periods of reduced hearing which can compromise the normal learning progress at a critical period in development.

But the diagnosis of SLD is usually given to children for whom there have been no obvious medical or environmental hazards and whose intelligence is not in the retarded range. Psychological assessment is the best medium for establishing diagnosis, and for providing assessment and analysis of the problem areas, but a multidisciplinary approach often including specialised speech and language assessment is always recommended to provide a complete picture. Details of diagnostic methods will be discussed in Chapter 4.

CAN WE PREDICT WHICH CHILDREN WILL DEVELOP SLDS?

There have been hundreds of studies aimed at finding predictors of SLDs. Children have been assessed in pre-school or very early primary school with measures that were believed to relate theoretically to "readiness", or which might tap into the necessary skills for successful learning. Some researchers have concentrated on physiological indicators, such as motor control and maturity as assessed for example with the "finger localisation" test, in which the child has to recognise which finger the examiner has touched when the child was not watching, or via copying and drawing skills.

Others have focused on linguistic measures such as letter knowledge, vocabulary, knowledge of sounds and rhymes in oral language, and the ability to build whole words from single sounds or syllables. Still others have put their faith in teacher ratings of readiness, or of the ability to follow instructions and remember what is taught, as well as pre-reading or early reading levels.

It is fair to say that none of the motor, sensory motor, or physiological measures has proved effective in picking out children who were likely to become SLD. Bradley and Bryant (1983) and others, have argued that rhyming ability is an important pre-reading skill and that children who begin school without this skill are at risk for reading problems. We know that children with early language delay or difficulties are at higher risk for SLDs although most of those who are of normal intelligence do quite well, and some children with no history of language delay nevertheless become LD. So prediction is not robust in this domain.

As will be explained in Chapter 6, attention problems and behavioural maladjustment evident before the child begins school puts the child at risk for SLDs.

A longitudinal study spanning 20 years carried out in the US by Baydar, Brooks-Gunn, and Furstenberg, (1993) found that pre-school cognitive and behavioural competencies strongly predicted literacy skills through to adulthood, even when the effects of socio-economic variables were taken into account. However, although such findings hold at a population sample level, it has been much harder to predict accurately which *individuals* will become SLD.

Teachers probably hold the best record for skill in prediction of children at risk for SLDs. If they are asked to rate specific skills involved in academic learning they are good at identifying children who are in difficulties, or who are likely to have problems. However even with their special knowledge it has to be said that prediction is still well below 100%.

To find good predictors is an ongoing challenge, because if we knew who was at risk, and why, we might be able to prevent later learning failure. The best conclusion based on current evidence is that general cognitive ability, language factors (particularly knowledge of letters, sounds, and rhymes), and attention/distractibility measures in the pre-school and early primary years, are the most useful predictors of the development of SLDs.

WHAT HAPPENS TO SLD CHILDREN?

The answer to this question depends on a complex mix of factors including: whether the child has associated behaviour problems; how early and how much remedial intervention is provided; how involved and active the parents are in helping the SLD child; social class and economic resources of the family; the level of intelligence of the child; relationships with teachers at school; the "resilience" of the child in the face of his or her difficulties. This latter factor is related to the child's temperament and ability to engage positively with people in his or her environment and to draw upon resources available to help. Children from lower socio-economic situations may be more likely to have a poorer outcome because they are likely to be multiply disadvantaged. Middle-class parents may be more able to access resources to help their child with SLDs. Children with behaviour problems are also much more handicapped in the long term.

In the short term, being SLD hinders all kinds of learning experiences for a child, leads to loss of confidence and self esteem, and may be associated with teasing and rejection by other children (and sometimes even the teacher). The gap between expected and actual achievement levels widens as the child moves up through primary school. Many children go into secondary school with literacy and numeracy levels that are at only a lower primary grade level. Hence they are extremely ill-equipped to cope with secondary school curricula. They are at high risk for absenteeism, getting into trouble, dropping out of school early, and seeing themselves as hopeless individuals. In the longer term, such students are at high risk for unemployment or low levels of employment, for psychosocial maladjustment and difficulties in handling even relatively simple everyday life tasks such as reading street signs, or instructions on medication. Follow-up of groups of SLD children into adulthood has found continuing handicap, unhappiness, maladjustment, and disadvantage, especially in cases where there was associated neurological handicap (Spreen, 1988). However a poor outcome is far from inevitable, with many individuals leading relatively comfortable and satisfying lives. Most studies of outcome indicate that early intervention must be the approach of first choice, as once children are set upon the SLD pathway, it is an enormous challenge to move them away from it.

The limited evidence on the longer-term outcome of RD children (Maughan, 1995) especially in non-referred or non-clinical samples confirms that RDs and SLDs are very persistent across the school years, and for many children the prognosis is poor in adolescence and adulthood. The likely consequences are: early school leaving, lower-paid employment, or unemployment; more mental health problems, and need for ongoing involvement with professional services. Reports from adults with RDs indicate the miseries of writing letters, filling in forms, trying to read street signs, phone books, filling in cheques etc.

However the outcome may be better for children from higher socio-economic status families with plenty of knowledge, assertiveness, and financial resources to help maximise the child's potential, although again the available data suggest that such influences are not particularly strong. The outcome is also better for those children who are very bright and who are thus able to develop high-level skills in other areas, or to compensate for their problems to some extent. It has been shown that such cases can go on to higher educational attainments even if they take longer than normal to reach their goals and have to focus on less reading-related areas of learning.

Delinquency is also associated with both early behaviour problems and SLDs, i.e. many children who get into trouble with the law have histories of school failure, and a proportion of those will be specifically LD. Anxiety, somatic complaints, and depression in adolescence and adulthood are also more common in SLD individuals (see Maughan, 1995, for review of this area).

For children with neurological problems, or with early language delay or disability, and for those with attention deficit hyperactivity disorder or conduct disorder in early childhood associated with SLDs, there is less chance that they will find compensating mechanisms to enhance their educational and employment outcome. Initial severity of the SLDs is also an important predictor of later progress; not surprisingly, the lighter the disability the better the prognosis. Boys and girls apparently do not differ in long-term outcome (Maughan, 1995). Continued efforts to improve reading skills are important; those children who persist with their education despite their difficulties continue to progress through adolescence and adulthood, and have a more positive outcome.

Even for those children who make a reasonably good "recovery" from RD, it is usually the case that they have enduring problems with spelling. Indeed this may be the only residual symptom in those cases with a good outcome.

In summary, SLDs are common problems in childhood, they tend to be stable, especially if they are not remediated early on, and they can lead to negative economic and psychosocial consequences in adolescence and adulthood. They are thus a significant community health problem.

ILLUSTRATIVE CASE HISTORY

Mark

Mark is 13 years old and is the youngest of four children in his family. His learning difficulties were first noticed when he was in Grade 1. He received some remedial help in Grade 3 but this had little apparent effect. Mark repeated Grade 4. At the time of referral and assessment, his Grade 6 teacher reports that he has difficulties in all areas, but English and Maths are the main concern with reading, spelling, and writing all very poor. Mark fails to complete set work and when he does do some it is usually very short, and very concrete and limited in its content.

Mark also has behavioural difficulties including problems with focusing and maintaining his attention, and remembering instructions and routines. He is disruptive in class and aggressive in the playground. Mark's father is very punitive towards him, believing that he does not work hard enough.

Psychological assessment showed that Mark's intelligence was in the normal range although he had severe problems with some sub-tests including: memory for a series of numbers, a task of written coding where he needed to process and remember a series of symbols to transcribe quickly, and comprehension of accepted social and moral behaviour . His reading and spelling were at about a 7.5-year-old level, i.e. below Grade 3 standard. He read hastily and in a mumble, with many mispronunciations and word substitutions. His mental and written arithmetic were slightly better than his reading, at about a Grade 4 level. However he often applied the wrong rule for the problem, and he was poor at using the correct sequential processes needed for problem solving. He did not check his answers.

Mark's writing was immature and poorly formed, he could not keep on a straight line without assistance and when asked to write a little story he could manage only two scarcely readable sentences. Neuropsychological tests of his memory capacities showed that he was able to recall structured meaningful material that he had learned quite well, but he could not devise his own strategies for learning in the absence of structure, and tried to rely on rote memory. Mark's visuomotor skills were very poor and tests showed that he had fine motor coordination problems, with writing and drawing skills all very impaired. His planning and organisation capacity on visual spatial tasks was well below that expected for his age.

Mark was clearly going to have severe problems with secondary-school-level work and it seemed an impossible task to equip him adequately in the few months of Grade 6 remaining to him. Keeping him in primary school for another year was not a good option as he was already a year older than his classmates. Although a remedial programme with two main emphases—increasing the store of words he could recognise and remember, and assistance with focusing and sustaining his attention—was essential, teachers also felt that a special programme tailored to Mark's needs should be set up for his first year in secondary school.

CHAPTER TWO

Reading and spelling problems

Within the broad field of LD, it is undoubtedly true that reading difficulties have attracted by far the greatest amount of attention. Billions of words have been written describing "dyslexia", reading retardation, reading disability, and specific reading difficulties, to name only a few of the terms that have been used. The volume of publications in the area signifies the intense interest it has aroused amongst scientists, health professionals, and educators, as well as within a variety of other disciplines. The focus of this chapter will be on a selective review of our understanding of how children learn to read and to spell, and on theories that try to explain why this learning process is abnormal for some children. Although comprehension may reasonably be argued to be the primary goal of reading, this cannot be achieved without single word reading ability. Little will be discussed in this chapter that is particularly concerned with comprehension processes, even though it is acknowledged that there can be RD children with adequate word recognition skills but poor comprehension, and that such children deserve attention and research. For the majority of children, it is problems in decoding words that hinder comprehension, hence the theory and knowledge in this area will be the prime focus for this overview.

HOW DO CHILDREN LEARN TO READ?

There are many models, theories, and descriptions of the ways in which children learn to read (see Marsh, Friedman, Welch, & Desberg, 1981, for an example). A number of theories are based on the notion of developmental, sequential "stages" in this learning process, which every child will experience in moving from beginning levels to the end goal of becoming a skilled reader.

These theories suggest that the earliest stage is one where children rely on visual contextual clues to guess at words—the "glance and guess" method. They also use particular *partial visual features*, especially first letters, as a recognition clue. If there are no helpful contextual clues, such as pictures, or story or character knowledge, the beginning reader cannot offer a response to an unfamiliar word.

The next stage, termed "sophisticated guessing" (Ellis, 1984), involves reading predominantly visually, on the basis of a growing store of known visual units. There is evidence of the use of visual similarity in the response to the word being read even if it is not exactly correct e.g. "plain" for "play". For normally progressing readers, there is a gradual increase in the sight vocabulary during this stage.

The next stage involves the acquisition of *grapheme–phoneme correspondences*, or "decoding", or "sounding out" rules that the child is either taught directly by parents or teachers, or succeeds in abstracting for himself and applying to new words. This works well for regular words such as "cab" which can be easily sounded out, but not well for more complex irregular words like "move" which would be sounded out as "m–o–v–ee", and be incomprehensible.

Successful acquisition of this phonemic (or letter–sound association) knowledge, allows children to achieve this stage, called *"alphabetic"* or *"phonic"*, in which they can apply grapheme (written symbol) to phoneme (sound symbol) correspondence rules to words, rather than relying on guessing. Hence at this stage they can make use of phonological processing skills.[1]

In the last, so-called *"orthographic"* stage, children use their increasingly sophisticated phonological knowledge in pronouncing orthographic sequences (e.g. syllables), and this is added to their mental bank of known words. Growing knowledge of rules, (for example, the rule of e at the end of the word which changes the sound of the middle vowel as in "line", also helps. At this level they become skilled readers (Frith, 1985).

Frith also proposes a stage model, which is an adaptation of the Marsh et al. (1981) model. In summary, it proposes: use of logographic (whole word storage and recognition); then alphabetic (letter–sound associations); then orthographic strategies (letter combinations corresponding to morphemes or word parts). The mastery of later stages is dependent on satisfactory attainment of earlier stages.

Frith (1985) also argues that in learning to *spell*, the alphabet strategies come *first* (not second as in reading), and thus spelling stages are not synchronous in development with reading stages. Nevertheless, the differently staged developmental learning pathways for reading and spelling enhance each other across the two domains.

RD arises when there is a failure to develop either one or the other system, or to move successfully from one stage to the next. The failure to achieve the move from logographic to alphabetic (roughly from stage 1 to stage 2), is seen as the most common key problem in reading disability. RD children often get stuck at the logographic stage; they do not develop the strategies necessary for the next stage, and thus cannot progress further at a normal rate.

Children may also develop strategies of reading by analogy especially if analogous relationships between words are pointed out to them (e.g. land is like sand), and if their stored vocabulary is good. But because of irregularities in the English language this does not always work; for example "come" is not like "home". Moreover, many RD children have impoverished vocabularies, they are just "not good with words", and so this strategy may not work well because they have trouble thinking of analogous words. A combination of a limited word store and an insecure grasp of decoding strategies is seriously handicapping. Phonological skills may fail to help a child if the sounded-out word does not find an association with a word in that child's vocabulary. Learning new whole words, or orthographic units, will also be handicapped if there is no match for the unit in the child's word memory bank; it will fail to access meaning.

---

[1] The following paragraph from Wagner, Torgesen, and Rashotte (1994, p.1) provides an excellent explanation of phonological processing as applied to the English language:

"Linguists have identified the set of basic sounds that individuals distinguish in ordinary conversation. There are from 30 to 45 of these basic sounds or Phonemes, depending on which classification system is being used. Every spoken word in English can be generated by combining these basic sounds, ... , only a relatively small number are used, and many of these combinations are common to more than one word. For example, two of the three basic sounds contained in the spoken words "cat" and "rat" are shared ... the basic sounds in common are represented by the shared letters, a and t, of their spellings. Presumably, some knowledge of the phonological structure of words such as "cat" and "rat" should be helpful when beginning readers attempt to learn their written forms. In particular, an awareness of phonemes may prove helpful in mastering an alphabet writing system such as English in which the letters correspond roughly to phonemes."

COGNITIVE ARCHITECTURE MODELS

So called "cognitive architecture" models have been developed and explicated by cognitive psychologists interested in exploring various models that try to explain how words are perceived, processed, and produced via hypothesised specific systems or "modules" in the brain. The Modular Information Processing Model of Ellis and Young (1988) for example, proposes first, that *input* systems for reading are different from *output* systems for spelling; and second, that there is a dual pathway for reading. Words can be recognised via *direct* visual (print) to semantic (meaning) systems; and also by *indirect*, letter–sound conversions (phonological decoding), and then via a second step, going from sound to meaning. This is known as the "dual route" theory of word recognition. Ellis (1984) describes reading by the direct visual route, (reading by eye), as the basis for the formation, through multiple encounters of the same word, of "visual word recognition units". Good readers develop a vast store of these units which are rapidly accessed in fluent reading. The indirect route, (reading by ear, or sound analysis), is a more cumbersome means of word recognition, but this letter to sound to word strategy is needed for unfamiliar words which do not activate a visual recognition unit in the individual"s word store. Remembering that RD children are characterised by limitations in their ability to recognise words (even after repeated presentations), they may have to rely more heavily on the phonological indirect route as an aid to finding the right print to word translation. The same comment, of course, applies to beginning readers, who have not had sufficient experience to build up a substantial sight vocabulary.

Spelling is analogous with the use of a mental dictionary of word forms to be "looked up", as well as a means of sound to letter translation (note that this "sound to print" pathway is in the opposite direction from the reading "print to sound" pathway). Thinking about reading and spelling processes on the basis of a cognitive architecture model provides a contrasting framework to the developmental stage approach. It focuses on the cognitive and linguistic modules or centres, which are hypothesised to exist in the brain and which are specialised for reading and spelling processes, and on the pathways that access meaning (reading or word recognition), and which produce written representations (written spelling).

Using this kind of model for assessment and remediation of RD suggests that if the particular impaired system or module could be identified, it could then be targeted for intervention, (treating the weakness). Alternatively, the least impaired system could be enhanced (emphasising the strengths).

So far though, there is limited empirical evidence to support direct connections between this modular approach to description and diagnosis of reading and spelling deficits, and the prescription of particular remedial methods. Seymour and Bunce (1994) used the cognitive architecture model to assess and analyse the specific aspects of RD in two boys and then to direct the focus of remediation based on their profiles. Their results highlighted the individual peculiarities of RD children in their problems, and in their reactions to remediation, rather than supporting a particular (modular) model of the reading process. Moving from theory to effective treatment in this field is quite a challenge.

Decoding skills

In a written alphabet based language such as English we need to learn a code, or a system of recognising the mappings between the printed symbols or letters, and the sounds they represent. Once a child learns this code he or she has a means of working out pronunciations of written words. Fluent readers who are familiar with the code do this automatically, so that reading is a smooth and relatively effortless process. They also build up a huge repertoire of known words which can be decoded instantly, and matched with, or referred to the inner "lexicon" or mental dictionary. Then meaning is accessed almost instantly via the direct visual route.

These processes apply to single word recognition, However in practice, children also use the context of what they are reading, e.g. picture illustrations, knowledge of the story, the setting, the characters, the probability of them behaving in certain ways, and regularities of grammar. Thus, in fluent reading the message is achieved on the basis of multiple cues, even though every single symbol may not be directly translated. Good readers have learned to respond to most words at a glance rather than having to decode them each time. It is also known that acquisition of these kinds of skills is affected to some extent by particular teaching methods, particularly in the early stages of learning to read, which may emphasise some strategies over others. For example, "whole language" approaches to reading stress a visual guessing strategy based on all the clues available, while phonological methods teach phoneme and word analysis strategies.

Children with reading disability have trouble breaking the code. They may be slow to learn the names and sounds of letters, how they blend together to form *phonemes*, or sound units (a–t = at; i–n = in; e–e = ee, etc.); how they go together into *syllable* units (ri–ding), or into *morphemes* or meaning units (find–ing). Often they are lacking in these early building blocks of code knowledge which they need in order to keep up with the reading material in the classroom. While they are still struggling to remember letters and simple sounds, their peers have gone on to succeed with words and sentences.

Decoding problems for RD children are clearly shown up when they are asked to spell and read non-words, such as "vib". As these are not actual words they rely heavily for pronunciation on the use of phonological skills. They have great difficulty in decoding the sounds or combinations of sounds in non-words to help them achieve a pronunciation, in a situation where there is no known word to which they can refer .

We know that these phonological decoding skills are critical to reading success, as early phonological abilities strongly predict later reading skills. Children who are slow or unable to develop these skills are very disadvantaged and are likely to always struggle with reading and spelling. They fall further and further behind. They do not then develop wide reading vocabularies; they are not motivated to keep trying to read because it is such an unrewarding effort; and they feel helpless about their chances of "cracking" the code. Hence disadvantage is piled on disadvantage.

This has been termed the "Matthew effect" in reading (Stanovich, 1986): "To them that hath shall be given, from them that hath not shall be taken away" (from the book of Matthew in the New Testament). In less biblical terms, the rich (good decoders) get richer, and the poor get poorer (fall further and further behind).

A number of studies in the US and in Europe (e.g. Goswami & Bryant, 1990; Wagner et al., 1994) have shown the reliability and stability of the relationship between early decoding and word recognition skills, and later reading achievement. Few children with these early decoding handicaps are able to "catch up" and become normal readers without special intensive intervention.

Many reading researchers have considered the question of cause and effect in the influence of phonological decoding skills. Much of this work is summarised and critically analysed in Goswami and Bryant's (1990) book *Phonological skills and learning to read*. Despite the evidence for strong relationships between early phonological skills and reading ability and disability, it cannot be claimed with certainty that one leads to the other, i.e. poor phonological skills "cause" a child to become RD, versus the alternative directional hypothesis: the RD child is disadvantaged because he or she does not learn such skills through increasing experience with print, hence RD leads to phonological problems. Nevertheless, Goswami and Bryant (1990) as well as other researchers assert that children's awareness of phonological attributes such as rhyme and alliteration in the early years can be shown to exert causal effects on reading skill development. There is not this same association with mathematical skills development, attesting to a degree of specificity of effects of phonological skills on reading (Shankweiler et al., 1995). Insensitivity to phonological units is characteristic of difficulties with learning to read. This is not to deny that experience with reading will also facilitate phonological skill development, so there is "two-way traffic" here.

Some teachers believe that most children who are slow to learn to read will catch up after some magic age milestone is reached (usually expected to be 8 years of age); and they may offer false comfort to worried parents by stating this belief. Evidence suggests that such a belief is not warranted. Children who are struggling to read even at a simple level after two or more years of instruction are likely to be still struggling on through primary and secondary school. This is not inevitable, because some children do make a late start, but manage to achieve an age-appropriate level somewhat later than usual. However it is unwise to take no remedial action in the hope that this will happen.

THE EARLY DEVELOPMENT OF PHONEMIC AWARENESS

A substantial majority of reading researchers believe that "phonemic awareness" is critical to success in reading. Phonemic awareness refers to the ability to discriminate, understand, and reflect upon the fact that words are made up of a series of sounds. It includes abilities such as recognising rhymes like cat and fat; knowing that cat has three specific but overlapping sounds within it, and recognising the existence of both similarities and differences in the constituent sounds of words, e.g. that cat and fat have much in common but also an important difference. This is awareness of onset "c" and rime "at", in a word. It also involves knowledge of the alphabetic principle, i.e. that there are systematic letter–sound correspondences. (One test of phonological awareness is to ask a child what is left if you take the "c" away from "cup".)

Children may develop phonological awareness in the early years, through word play, nursery rhymes, and following the reading of storybooks with parents. The development of this capacity is very helpful in preparing children to learn to read. It can also be specifically taught to young children, with positive effects on their later reading and spelling achievement (see Bradley & Bryant 1983; Bryant & Bradley 1985). Knowledge of rhymes in the pre-school period is associated with better early reading achievement. Knowing that words such as "cat", "bat", and "mat" rhyme, can help the child to read and spell "fat" by analogy, and teaches about the rules and regularities, (or irregularities) of the language.

Debate continues about whether the early development of phonological awareness skills provides beneficial "precursors" to good reading, and to what extent such skills develop alongside, or as a consequence of reading practice. Goswami and Bryant (1990) for example suggest that the awareness of word onset and rime, as in "br" (onset) and "ing" (rime) = br/ing, which is easier than phonemic segmentation, might be the crucial element in learning to read. Knowledge of smaller units or phonemes is more difficult to achieve and can develop as a consequence of reading experience.

It is probably reasonable to conclude on the basis of current evidence that although the beneficial effects can and do go in both directions, early phonological skills are certainly predictive of good reading, and a lack of phonological skills is predictive of reading difficulties. Moreover, phonological processing skills are extremely stable and consistent from pre-school to later years. Although many older RD children will have developed some level of skill which helps them to progress, children with severe reading problems find it hard to learn and retain phonological skills even when they are specifically taught. For some this can be a real "deficit", rather than a "developmental delay" in catching on. As noted in the previous chapter, there is also evidence that the inherited aspect of RD appears to be phonological skill capacities, so it is clear that this capacity is of central importance in reading theory and practice.

A lack of phonemic awareness skills can show up in young children"s early attempts to spell. Mis-spellings often reflect phonological knowledge, with phonemically aware children producing attempts that sound quite like the correct word, and phonemically unaware children providing wild guesses, with combination of letters that do not make any "sound" sense (e.g. rur for rain).

Experimental studies of phonemic segmentation skill and spelling strategies support claims that children with spelling difficulties are deficient in using phonology in the adaptive way that non-disabled children can, when trying to spell new words (see Snowling, 1991).

It is not true, however, that every RD child has problems with phonological processing, so the links are not absolute. Castles and Coltheart (1993), and others, have shown that some RD children can read non-words (like "vib") reasonably well, suggesting that they do have phonological skills, even though their reading of real words, especially *irregular* words may be very impaired. That is, their visual word-recognition skills are limited, and their phonological knowledge, although present, has not been enough to compensate for their limitation and bring their reading up to a normal level.

Linking back to the dual route theory noted earlier, which grew out of psycholinguistic studies of acquired dyslexic cases, researchers have argued that such results suggest that there are at least two types of developmental reading disability. One type occurs when the phonological or indirect route is intact but the direct visual route is impaired. This is called "surface dyslexia" which is the name given to the *acquired* reading disorder that has similar reading-related symptoms. The symptoms include relative facility with reading *regular* words which can be sounded out (an example is "help"), along with problems in reading *irregular* words (these include "exception" words that do not follow the usual rules of pronunciation, such as "have" which is more usually pronounced as in "gave"; and ambiguous words such as those containing "own" or "ough" which vary in their sounds in an unpredictable fashion); and a tendency to "regularise" irregular words or try ineffectively to sound them out.

The other type of RD occurs when the phonological route is impaired but the direct visual route, if not intact, is at least stronger than the other indirect route. This is called "phonological dyslexia" which is the name given to the acquired disorder that has similar symptoms, such as facility with reading both regular and irregular words which can be read via the direct route, but difficulties with non-words (e.g. "hif"), or rare words (e.g. "flora") where phonological strategies, or use of the indirect route, are needed.

Findings with developmental cases have been argued to support the "dual route" theoretical approach to reading (Snowling, 1991), and to suggest that there are some important cognitive neuropsychological differences between RD individuals of different types. Such evidence may also fit alongside the stage models of reading outlined earlier, in that the breakdown in the process of learning to read may occur at different points, leaving some children stalled at the *logographic* stage, who should theoretically be worse readers than those stalled at the second *alphabetic* stage, as the latter are further along the pathway to skilled reading. There is some evidence for this latter claim from a remedial study by Prior, Frye, and Fletcher (1987), who found that children with weak phonological skills (stalled at the logographic stage) profited least from remediation, simply because they had fewer strategies to apply to their reading attempts and were more handicapped than those who had some phonological abilities.

A great deal of the evidence relevant to theories of differing routes to single word reading has come from studies of non-word reading. Having to read a non-word (a pseudoword such as "plem"), it is argued, must provide a way into understanding of how one reads, as these non-words are obviously unfamiliar and must be accessed for the first time.

Non-word reading is claimed to give a direct indication of phonological skills, which have been shown to be notably deficient in RD children in many studies. Findings of such deficits are not inevitable, however. Rack, Snowling, and Olson (1992), found no evidence for specific phonological problems in one third of the large number of studies of non-word reading they reviewed. In trying to explain the lack of uniformity in the findings, Rack et al. (1992) suggested that the age of the children tested was important (the younger the child, whether RD or not, the greater the difficulty in reading non-words); the level of complexity of the non-words exerts an influence (some simpler varieties can be read by analogy with real words); there may be priming effects with non-words that are similar to real words, (e.g. "rin"), triggering the use of a visual analogy, rather than a phonological strategy; and the methods used to match children on reading age and intelligence may also explain some of the discrepancies.

Although much current argument rests on the belief that the "phonological deficit" theory of RD is the best explanation for observed problems (see Share, 1995), it must be conceded that the great majority of RD children are handicapped in the use of *both* direct visual whole word and indirect phonological strategies. These routes operate effectively in tandem in skilled reading, but are out of balance in RD children. Some children who read mostly by whole word visual strategies still show evidence for some phonological abilities in their written spelling. So this is not an all or nothing phenomenon—most children have some elements of both strategies. Rack et al. (1992) suggest that there will be differing combinations and levels of phonological and whole word skills at different ages in different children. Individual differences rather than sub-types or categories are a more realistic framework for considering the strengths and deficits of RD children.

THE TEACHING OF READING

In the past, young children received some phonics training in the classroom. However in the last 50 years or so, the "whole word" or "look say" or "language awareness" approaches have come to dominate the teaching of reading in many Western cultures. This view suggests that children should be encouraged to make guesses about a word, based on as many clues as they can pick up from the print and its context, without necessarily applying decoding or sub-word analysis strategies. It is a "top down" approach to learning to read.

Despite research demonstrating the importance of phonological knowledge in reading and spelling (Beck & Juel, 1992), many education systems dominated by "whole word" philosophy, have been reluctant to change their pedagogical policies which are often based more on "received wisdom" or politically driven philosophies than on empirical findings. Indeed a number of eminent reading researchers have bemoaned the fact that the large body of research findings that has illuminated our knowledge of reading success and failure, has failed to penetrate the curricula of teacher training institutions.

In fact, most children learn to read adequately no matter what teaching methods they experience. But our concern is with that percentage who fail to learn to read and spell, and for whom the "look say" or whole word/top down approach has clearly been ineffective. RD children have not "naturally" developed phonological skills as do non-RD children, and therefore they will require extra induction of strategies to help them to make sense of print (see Chapters 7 and 8 in reference to remedial methods).

Although grapheme–phoneme translation skills are stressed here as essential building blocks for skilled reading, and as a critical area of handicap in children who fail at reading, the argument that a whole language approach should dominate the teaching and learning of reading even for RD children, should not be totally discarded. It does not seem to disadvantage the majority of children in the classroom, and it is intuitively more appealing than "bottom up" or specific word analysis methods, which may be less engaging for young children. And it may be that for some RD children with stronger whole word visual recognition skills, and for whom the learning of phonics remains a major obstacle, it is better to capitalise on their strengths in using this approach.

However, there is little evidence to support any claim that this whole language teaching method is sufficient for children who fail to follow the normal path to skilled reading. Their needs must be catered for with teaching methods that facilitate the acquisition of phonological strategies.

VISUAL PROCESSES IN READING

Despite the views presented here arguing for the central importance of phonological skills in reading and reading disability, this is not the whole story. Much research has focused on the role and significance of visual factors in reading and spelling.

Historically, there has been a strong tendency to search for a single underlying causal factor for RDs. Early theories of RD placed considerable emphasis on visual factors as likely candidates in the search for causes, although these theories have diminished in salience as research has more and more centred on language, especially phonological, factors. But, bearing in mind the heterogeneity of LD children, and the likelihood of not a single but multiple interacting causes for SLDs, it is foolish to take an either/or position regarding visual versus phonological bases of RDs. Both processes are involved in reading.

It is possible to have perfectly normal visual functioning in every aspect of life but still struggle with print; and to have reasonable phonological skills but still fail to recognise words that ought to be well known; or to have problems in differentiating between "figure" and "ground" (target letters or words, and the surrounding space). In fact, one mother reported to me that it was after some years of struggling to read that her RD son told her he had only recently realised that it was the "black bits" rather than the "white bits" that were the key features. Although this is an unusual case, it reminds us that for some children, visual discrimination and visual memory processes may present problems, and that it would be unwise to dismiss such factors or to exclude them from further research into LDs.

It is impossible to do justice to the research in this area in a brief review. However, readers who wish to probe further into the influence of visual factors will find valuable, up to date summaries in a review of this field by Willows, Kruk, and Corcos (1993).

Opinion remains divided about whether RD and normal readers differ in their processing of visual information. The weight of current opinion, however, suggests that visual deficits are only apparent in RD children when *linguistic* stimuli are being processed, hence implicating language rather than purely visual factors (Vellutino, 1979).

One important question is whether any visual deficits that might be identified in RD children are *cause* or *effect* of their reading problems. Perhaps such children develop abnormal visual scanning and processing habits as a reaction to their difficulties with print. This is a difficult question to answer without large sample, longitudinal studies that can examine which characteristics precede which, in the development of learning skills in young children. Moreover, visual problems, if they are found in experimental studies, may be a reflection of broader capacities or deficiencies such as attentional processes, visual memory, or speed of information processing, rather than basic visual perceptual problems.

Bryant and Impey (1986) have shown that individual differences in the balance of visual and linguistic strengths and deficits are apparent in normally reading children, i.e. are not associated with learning difficulties *per se*. Studies using comparison groups of normally reading children will usually find some children who show visual perceptual weaknesses of the same kind as can be found in RD children. Hence there is nothing specific about such problems which might help to explain RD.

A variety of clinical and experimental approaches to examining the significance of visual factors in RD have been tried. Since the 1960s there have been a number of sub-typing studies in which batteries of language and visuo-spatial tests have been administered to SLD children to search for subgroups that may share similar deficits and perhaps similar causes. In some of this research, subgroups of children whose problems seemed to be rather more visual than linguistic have been identified. But it is difficult to draw general conclusions from such studies because of wide variation in the criteria for SLD used in selection of subjects, and the diversity in the batteries of achievement, and diagnostic and experimental tests used to attempt to differentiate subgroups.

Nevertheless, many studies report finding a cluster of children who do more poorly on visual perceptual tasks and who are relatively much stronger on auditory/linguistic tasks (see Chapter 5). Few of them, however, are without any auditory-linguistic deficits. It may be that visual processing problems can *contribute* to failure to learn to read competently for some children, although there is no evidence that they are either a *necessary or a sufficient* cause of RD. There is also the challenge of explaining how any visual or perceptual anomalies that are found could translate into the specific word recognition and word memory problems of the RD child.

Visual processing problems could be a *consequence* of difficulty in learning to read which leads children to all kinds of maladaptive and inconsistent scanning strategies as they try to make sense of print. This uncertainty about cause versus effect, and the nature of any influence of visual factors, means that claims to remediate reading problems using visually based programmes are premature at the very least.

In a recent critical review of this area, Garzia (1993) was unable to provide any conclusions about the specific contributions of visual (optometric) factors in RD, because of problems with subject definition and selection, and methods of specifying and diagnosing relevant visual defects in the published research literature. He suggested that correction of visual deficits is more likely to be relevant for less disabled (as compared with specific RD or dyslexic type) readers. He also drew attention to the influence of motivation, and of the development of different visual scanning strategies perhaps as a consequence of experience of RD. Nevertheless, it is important to screen for vision defects if there are any indications of such problems in the LD child.

It is of interest to note that there is evidence that three famous artists with undoubted gifts in visual processing and memory skills showed signs of being "dyslexic". These were Leonardo da Vinci, who showed spelling errors similar to those found in dyslexic cases, which were unlikely to be the consequence of limited schooling or historical differences in acceptable spelling (Sartori 1987, cited in Willows et al. 1993); Auguste Rodin, the brilliant sculptor who was reported to have had great difficulty learning to read and write, and remained handicapped in this area in adulthood, needing secretaries to read and write for him; and the American painter Charles Russell, for whom records of letters show him to have had very poor spelling, syntax, and punctuation.

SPELLING DIFFICULTIES

Writing and spelling problems have been called "dysgraphia" or literally, abnormal writing. They have been relatively little studied by comparison with RD (but see Frith, 1980), although of course the processes involved in reading and spelling are closely associated, and most theories of reading, including those outlined in this chapter, will incorporate the learning of spelling into their models, (e.g. Frith, 1985). "Acquired dysgraphia" like acquired dyslexia has been studied in adults. Although this term literally means abnormal writing, it usually refers to spelling problems rather than being concerned with the motor act of actually putting down letters or words onto a page.

Reading and spelling are highly related abilities with estimates of correlations ranging between .5 and .8 (Aaron, 1982). Almost every RD child will have similar or even greater difficulties with spelling. However not all poor spellers are also poor readers—there is considerable variance between the two input and output processes.

With normal children, Bryant and Bradley (1980) have shown that youngsters learning to read and write can spell some words that they fail to read correctly, and vice versa. Their study provided some evidence that at this early stage children preferred a visual reading strategy, but used phonological strategies to assemble spelling. They could, however, be induced to change strategies depending on the context. For example, they could successfully read regular words they had previously not known when they were part of a text of non-words for which phonic strategies had to be brought into play.

Learning to spell, then, is not the same as learning to read. Hence we need to know how it is that children learn, or fail to learn, how to produce the correct string of letters which represents the word they want to write.

Theories of spelling acquisition

Early theories of spelling such as that of Luria (1970) were based on the belief that spelling was phonically mediated; i.e. came about by literal translation of the spoken sound of the word into a written representation. But, as with similar uni-dimensional theories of reading, this notion is inadequate to explain correct spelling, particularly when it comes to irregular words, whose components do not translate exactly into the correct sound of the word. It also fails to account for the correct spelling of "homophones" i.e. words that sound the same but look different and differ in meaning, e.g. rain/reign, saw/sore, son/sun, etc.

Goswami and Bryant (1990) argue that children rely very much on phonological skills when trying to spell a word they do not know, and that there is no logographic stage in children"s learning of spelling as there is in reading. They argue for a distinction between the processes of learning to read and to spell. Other supporting research data have shown that children who are poor spellers also perform poorly in phonological tasks; and as noted earlier, phonological and spelling skills appear to have the strongest level of heritability by comparison with other aspects of literacy skills, attesting to their integral connections.

One has to be careful with the literature on this topic to judge whether one is thinking about "learning to spell" where indeed there is good evidence for reliance on phonology; or whether the issue is: what do more and less skilled spellers produce, some time after the initial learning stages—or, what characterises good versus poor spelling? Children with spelling (and usually reading) problems can get stuck at the phonology stage and do not move on to develop and use a securely known store of word spellings, spelling rules and conventions. However, the SLD child struggling with spelling, who has phonological translation skills that he or she can apply to spelling is better off than the purely "visual" (guessing) speller, because at least he or she will produce a representation that can be understood.

Two charming examples from Read"s (1986) book *Children"s creative spelling* illustrate this point (p.130):

"My Dadaay wrx hir"
"B cwyit".

The phonic mediation theory does explain why children often produce phonetically correct spelling such as brane for brain, and why regular words are more likely to be spelled correctly than irregular words. But with time and experience, most children learn the word-specific spellings, and do not need to rely on phonic methods. The good speller rarely makes phonetic-type errors, although the SLD child may continue to do so, alongside frequent bizarre guessing attempts. Because English spelling is so often irregular, *competent* spelling relies on accessing a stored memory for a whole word; then the written form must be visually rather than auditorily checked against that representation, (Ellis, 1984).

Children with well-developed skills access correct spellings from the store they accumulate in memory as they learn. That is, there is a kind of spelling dictionary which is mentally "looked up" to achieve a correct written form of each word. Children who fail to accumulate a mental dictionary of correct spellings, or whose store is very limited, may try to spell words they cannot "look up" successfully by using phonemic translation methods. Using this strategy they often come close to the appropriate translation and we can usually understand what it is they are trying to write (krless for koalas, feree for very, terabal for terrible). Others may remember a few of the relevant letters but get them in the wrong order (e.g. cklu for cruel), or add a few unwanted letters, or leave out some (dot for don"t). Poor spellers then do not check what they have written to see if it makes sense, or they do not read their spelling for detail and may only focus on salient letters (such as the first, middle, or last). Some kinds of guessed spellings are often impossible to understand (e.g. fyest for fire, garfara for giraffe, or efones for elephants). In such examples, the child seems to access some of the relevant letters, especially the first one which is often correct, but they cannot remember how the word they want should look.

Another means that children sometimes use to access spelling is by analogy with a word that is accurately known (Frith, 1985), perhaps by rhyme or by a salient feature, e.g. producing the wrong spelling for "said" by using the rhyme of "head" which gives you "sead". It is also hard in spelling to remember whether there are double letters such as two "r"s, as for example in "correct", or which vowel belongs in the last syllable of words like eminence, and resistance. These are essentially conventions that make it hard to get words correct by the application of rules. Even good spellers will make these kinds of errors sometimes, suggesting that their word-specific memory can be less than completely accurate.

The dual route model has also been applied to the understanding of spelling. Using the *indirect* print to sound translation route will predispose to phonological errors when spelling is incorrect. The errors of good spellers are actually more likely to be of this type, as they try a phonological strategy when they cannot accurately recall the correct representation. Use (or mis-use) of the *direct*, visual to meaning route in LD children leads to the kinds of errors described earlier (e.g. fyest), which are very difficult to understand because there is so little in common between the correct and incorrect spelling to provide clues.

Nevertheless, although reading and spelling/writing are closely associated processes it may be argued that the cognitive mechanisms for achieving "heard" representations (reading aloud or silently), and written, "seen", representations of words are somewhat different. Frith (1985) has argued that the two sets of skills develop along somewhat different pathways. There are inconsistencies in reading and spelling knowledge and strategies, and as the next section will show, it is possible to be a good reader and a poor speller. Nevertheless, children with RD almost inevitably have problems with spelling. Indeed the most common pattern found is that spelling is worse than reading. Furthermore, when RD children do make good progress towards a normal level of literacy, it is common for them to have continuing and intransigent difficulties with spelling. Spelling problems seem more resistant to the processes of teaching and remediation strategies, and it is much harder to get improvement. This may be for a variety of reasons. Children may have less practice in writing than reading and may be more successful in avoiding it; it may be less emphasized by teachers and parents as they focus their efforts on trying to help the SLD child to master reading; or it may be that *producing* a correct word from one"s mental spelling dictionary is harder than *recognising* one in print, especially where there are plenty of contextual clues.

Specific spelling difficulties (SSD)

There are some children who read perfectly well but have specific spelling problems. Again this is a deficit not explicable by reference to intelligence, educational opportunity, or sensory problems. Such children are sometimes called "developmentally dysgraphic", meaning that they cannot learn to write words accurately. This rather cumbersome term is taken from the adult literature where there are examples of normally literate adults who lose the ability to spell and write correctly, after some kind of brain trauma. There is little information about the prevalence of SSD but McCorriston (1991) found 3% of children in normal primary schools in Australia who were good readers but poor spellers. This is about the percentage one would expect to find, given that there is a normal distribution of spelling skill in a population of normally intelligent children where reading and spelling are correlated at about .7. There is some evidence that SSD children are less likely to have the lower verbal IQ that is sometimes found in children with spelling and reading problems, perhaps supporting the notion that this is a problem that is somewhat different from the spelling difficulties which are associated with RD. Nelson and Warrington (1974) showed that SSD children had normal verbal skills, whereas the group with both reading and spelling difficulties showed some evidence of language impairment. The two groups of children also varied in the *types* of errors they made, with SSD children producing a larger number of phonetically accurate errors. Nelson and Warrington suggested different causes for the spelling problems in the two groups.

However, McCorriston's (1991) investigation of the characteristics of good readers/poor spellers, and poor readers/poor spellers, found that apart from rather better grapheme–phoneme knowledge in the former group, there were essentially no differences between them in the spelling or any other domain. She concluded that SSD children may not constitute a particular "unexpected" or "pathological" group with particular associated linguistiç impairments, or that there is a specific "dysgraphia" syndrome. This was an unexpected finding because Frith (1980) had shown in a series of experiments that SSD children consistently showed poorer letter to sound conversion skills in reading, and were slower readers. However McCorriston and McKenzie (1981) showed that these same SSD children, when compared with competent readers and spellers, were more likely to use visual strategies, and were more error-prone when they were forced to use phonological analysis strategies. This is more consistent with the Frith (1978a) findings.

Children with SSD have failed to adequately learn the kinds of word-specific rules that govern the production of written representations, especially in a language as complex and irregular as English. They are likely to spell phonetically (e.g. brooz for bruise), so that the word can be pronounced but is not correct by traditional spelling. Without this word-specific knowledge we cannot spell irregular words like "friend", "yacht", and "knowledge". Similar deficits are found in children with the combination of reading and spelling difficulties. They are not confined to any one SLD group. It is also claimed that children with SSD make fewer of the bizarre non-phonetic errors sometimes produced by reading-disabled children, probably because they have somewhat better phonological translation skills.

Both groups also make spelling errors typical of very young children learning to spell, so it is as if they have become stuck at an early level. They seem less able to develop strategies to foster the normal increase in the bank of known spellings which enable children to move on to acquire a large, reliable reservoir of word-specific spelling knowledge.

Frith (1978) has noted the relative neglect of spelling difficulties, from both a theoretical and practical point of view. Although her (1980) book redressed the neglect to some extent, there is still much to be learned about this process and about helpful remedial measures.

Remedial reading programmes may not be sufficient to aid progress with spelling. Specific approaches to spelling remediation, including attention to the details of letters and phonemes, to rules for correct spelling, and to checking of written words, will be essential. Emphasis on output in the form of repeated writing practice with single words and with connected prose will also be needed. This is quite a challenge because children with spelling problems have often become reluctant writers and need special encouragement to keep trying. Some remedial methods for spelling, such as "Simultaneous Oral Spelling", reviewed in Chapter 8, emphasise multi-sensory strategies; auditory, visual, and kinaesthetic in combination with repetitive practice. This approach tries to bring into play as many integrated strategies as possible in an attempt to "cement in" correct spellings.

SUMMARY

Understanding the cognitive mechanisms for spelling and reading is essential if we are to find effective ways of helping individuals who do not develop the normally smooth and relatively effortless pathways to print recognition and production. Useful sources of evidence about skill acquisition have come both from developmental studies of young children learning to read and spell, and from studying the errors made by adults who have "acquired" reading or spelling disorders. Experimental studies of normal people, in which researchers try to demonstrate how words are accessed under specific controlled conditions in the laboratory, have also provided insight into the ways in which cognitive linguistic processes operate in the brain. However although some general psycholinguistic theories are very useful in studying these processes, the enormous individual differences between people, and particularly within a population of SLD children, and the amazing flexibility of the brain to process information even when it is degraded or manipulated in strange ways, make it difficult to identify one theory that satisfactorily explains all possible reading and spelling performance. It is reasonable to conclude, though, that the weight of current evidence supports first, the central importance of phonological knowledge in learning to read and to spell, and second, the need for reading and spelling difficulties to *each* be treated in the LD child.

In summary, this chapter has provided a brief outline of some of the major issues, problems, and research endeavours concerned with reading and spelling processes. There are very many up to date published papers and books which offer much more detailed analyses of a very complex field, some of which have been cited here, and which can be followed up by readers seeking more in-depth theoretical knowledge and research data.

In this outline it has been suggested that stage models—which explicate the ways in which children"s early reading skills develop from logographic or visual guessing strategies, through alphabetic or phonological decoding attempts, to orthographic or word unit processing strategies which lead to skilled reading—are helpful in understanding how breakdown in the process may occur for RD individuals. Cognitive architectural models have also contributed greatly to an understanding of the pathways from print to meaning (reading), and from word meaning to written spelling, and the dual route theory that dominates this area was described (see Coltheart & Rastle, 1994, for recent evidence on dual route models). There has been considerable emphasis in this chapter on phonological awareness and phonological skill development, stemming from the conviction that these are central to the understanding of reading and spelling abilities and disabilities. Phonological skills are predictive of reading competence, they are characteristic of good readers, and lack of phonological skills underlies the failure to master reading in a substantial proportion, if not the majority of cases of RD (Share, 1995). Although visual processes are not unimportant in reading, it was argued that problems in such processes offer relatively little that is particularly helpful in understanding or remediating RD.

Spelling difficulties are less well understood by comparison with RD and existing findings are rather inconsistent.

CHAPTER THREE

Problems with mathematics

ILLUSTRATIVE CASE HISTORY

Brian is a 13 year old boy in the second year of secondary school who was referred by his teacher for assessment because of his difficulties with maths and his poor concentration.

His developmental history was uneventful although Brian was described as a rather socially isolated child. Despite having special help from his father, Brian could not retain the rules used in arithmetic calculation. He was a good reader and his intelligence was in the average range, with his weakest scores on mental arithmetic, and on memory for a string of numbers. Neuropsychological testing showed that his auditory-verbal memory span was somewhat below age expected level, but he was able to learn and remember connected and structured material such as sentences and stories. His visual memory was below average. Brian's spelling was very poor and may be related to his difficulties with remembering visual material. He used phonological strategies to help write more complex words.

To comprehensively assess his mathematical difficulties Brian was given the Keymath–R test which showed him to be overall more than one standard deviation below the average for 13-year-olds. The poorest area of functioning was in "Operations" which measures computational skills including addition, subtraction, division, and multiplication, as well as mental computation of orally and visually presented problems. His knowledge of fractions, decimals, percentages, and spatial relations was not much below average, but he was handicapped in the *application* of mathematics such as in Time and Money tests, where the ability to use the clock, calendar, coins, currency values, and simple money management are tested. Brian's memory weakness seemed relevant to many of his difficulties; he could not reliably remember how to apply computational routines, and lacked confidence in everyday skills because he worried about whether he was recalling the correct strategies. It is likely that visual memory deficits for symbolic material were common to Brian's problems in reproducing correct spellings and in remembering rules to be applied to new problems. However there was nothing in his developmental history that might have explained why these specific problems had arisen, while reading was unimpaired. Perhaps his phonological skills were major compensating factors in his reading competence.

Brian's poor spelling skills and delayed development of everyday "life skills" as for example in telling the time, and in using money, needed intensive focused remedial work. This included prescription of multisensory strategies for learning and remembering the *look* of words in print, so that he could check his spelling attempts; instruction and practice in telling the time; and concrete, supervised experience in managing real-life money matters in his environment. Recommendations for remedial assistance took into account Brian's limitations in the ability to spontaneously extract important visual cues from the material he needed to learn, and to organise nonverbal information. Making use of auditory verbal along with visual presentation of material was recommended, along with the need for more time to process and remember information, and for more highly organised meaningful structure in the information presented. Special supervised provision of frequent opportunities to go over the material he was studying was suggested. Plenty of praise and encouragement for even small successes was recommended to build up Brian's confidence in his maths skills, and his motivation to sustain his attention during maths lessons in the classroom.

INTRODUCTION

Difficulties with arithmetic, or calculating, or knowledge of mathematical processes, which can be called "numeracy", are found in more than one child in every classroom. However these problems have been very little studied by comparison with reading difficulties and it is not really known how common they are. This may be because such difficulties are less apparent in the early years of school than are reading problems, and tend to go unnoticed for longer. Or it may be that mathematical abilities are perceived as less critical for educational and occupational success in the longer term compared with literacy skills, i.e. that maths skills are perhaps socially less valued, so that failure in this area is less stigmatising for children and adults. In fact, nobody seems upset when people say they are "hopeless with numbers", whereas failure to be able to read is something people try to hide.

However, many children finish school with less than adequate competence in and negative attitudes towards mathematics, and many adults feel inadequate and anxious when they are obliged to call upon their numeracy skills. Adults with poor numeracy skills often find strategies to conceal their difficulties. For example, in managing change, they will simply accept what they are given, or always try to purchase in such a way that they will not need to cope with change. The widespread availability of calculators has made life easier for those who feel slow or inadequate with calculations, but this does not obviate the need for grasping the processes involved in solving maths problems, and in acquiring the understanding and skills that allow one to use calculators as effective tools. It is first necessary to translate the problem or the calculation into the correct mathematical form before calculators can be put to use.

There are two bodies of literature that can inform our understanding of mathematical difficulties. The first is that coming primarily from the educational psychology discipline where the learning and performance of children as they develop maths skills, from very simple levels to more complex skills, has been studied (see, for example, Bryant, 1995; Fuson, 1984, 1986; Hughes, 1986; Murray & Mayer 1988). This has contributed much knowledge of the developmental pathways in problem-solving strategies in arithmetic especially. It has shown that mastery of basic arithmetic underpins the learning of more complex mathematical capacities which depend on accurate memory for basic facts. The *Journal for Research in Mathematics Education* is a useful source of this genre of research.

The second body of literature comes from studies of individuals who have lost the ability to calculate as a consequence of brain damage of some kind; this work parallels but is less extensive than that concerned with the cognitive neuropsychology of acquired reading difficulties. There ought to be an additional literature parallel to that for RD, where developmental theory and in-depth study of children suffering from mathematical problems is brought together to provide useful theory about the nature and origins of the difficulties. However, such work is quite scarce by comparison with that available for RD and theory has been slower to develop (but see Geary, 1993). Consequently much of the discussion in this chapter on mathematical difficulties remains at a descriptive level.

DYSCALCULIA

Most of the original research into "arithmetic disorders" was carried out by studying adults who had sustained some kind of brain damage from bullet wounds or tumours, and had *lost* the ability to calculate. This has been called "dyscalculia" (see Luria 1966). Farnham-Diggory (1978, p.90) has described one of Luria's patients who was previously a skilled calculator but became dyscalculic after a bullet wound. Some of the scant theory about numeracy problems in childhood has been derived from the clinical literature. However, as we are dealing for the most part with a "developmental" disorder and not an "acquired" one, there is need to take a developmental learning perspective rather than a "pathology" perspective to understand problems in this area. By developmental disorder is meant problems that seem to begin in the early years of life and result in delay or deficits in acquiring certain skills; or, put another way, an inadequate level of skill given the child's age and background experience, including exposure to satisfactory teaching.

It is uncertain to what extent numeracy problems occur as a single LD in children. A small number of children show specific problems with reasoning and/or with computational processes in maths. However it is common for RD children to also have problems with maths, either because they have LDs encompassing the three Rs, or because their language and reading difficulties handicap them in reading and understanding maths questions and problems, and hence they are unable to discover what they are meant to do.

However mathematics involves a wide range of diverse skills so that, potentially, various combinations of problems may occur in a population of SLD children. It is likely that it would be rare for a child to show "purely" problems confined to mathematics. Many of the difficulties seen in RD children, such as memory for the order of letters or failure to develop a set of rules that may be applied to translate new words from print to sound, are likely to also impinge on mathematics ability. Many RD children show a lack of knowledge of fundamental operations in mathematics which seems to be related to other aspects of their LDs. Furthermore, research has shown that many of the same ability factors in kindergarten children which correlate with later reading abilities also correlate with arithmetic skills, demonstrating the commonality of at least some of the underlying skills and learning processes.

It has been claimed that children with verbal memory problems are vulnerable to difficulties with arithmetic. Verbal memory problems are also common in RD children; hence this may be one common underlying factor in the presence of LDs in several areas, in many children. So, in a large proportion of SLD children, poor arithmetic skills may be a consequence of the same factors that are associated with poor reading.

It is unclear whether numeracy problems have a similar level of heritability to that found in reading problems, as there is little research into this question. There were some early studies of twins and of familial resemblance in mathematical abilities (Geary, 1993), but these have not disentangled the likely common influences on reading and mathematics abilities, nor the question of whether MD (Mathematical Difficulties) can be considered a specific disorder (as for example parallel to "dyslexia"), or the lower end of the distribution of mathematical abilities. The same arguments that were outlined in Chapter 1 concerning reading and its distribution in the population apply to mathematics. Behaviour-genetic studies which try to separate out various components and sub-types of MD and look at possible mechanisms of inheritance as has been done in the genetic studies linking phonological skill heritability to RD, are very much needed.

Whether clear neuropsychological associations can be established in developmental cases, as they have been in adult "acquired" cases of "dyscalculia" where site of injury is associated with types of deficit, is another question on which there is little information.

PREVALENCE OF MD

It is not easy to estimate how many children have MD because we do not have a standard agreed definition of the problem. It is possible to use deviations from what is expected on the basis of intelligence level and age/grade as we do in defining reading disability. The age at which children become competent in various forms of calculation varies considerably. O'Hare, Brown, and Aitken (1991) suggest that if a child cannot add and subtract without the help of concrete aids by the age of 7+ years, and cannot do simple multiplication by the age of 10½ , or cannot do division by 13, then he or she is "dyscalculic". This is a helpful rule of thumb but has no systematic evidence of validity.

A number of authors have suggested a prevalence of MD of around 6% of the school-aged population. For example, Badian (1983) reported that 6.4% of children in Grades 1 to 8 in a small US town showed poor achievement in maths, compared to 5% with reading problems. More than half of the RD children were also behind in maths, and almost half of the MD children were poor at reading. Shalev et al. (1995) studied a substantial group of Israeli children who were two years behind in arithmetic in Grade 4. Although epidemiological data were not reported, they found no gender differences in a sub-group of the original sample studied at the age of 11–12 years and they reported that 17% also had reading problems.

In a recent British epidemiological study of 9–10-year-olds, Lewis, Hitch, and Walker (1994) found that 2.3% of children had combined reading and arithmetic problems, 3.9% had specific reading problems, and 1.3% had specific arithmetic disorders. The sex ratio was approximately equivalent in the specific and the combined problem groups. Fletcher and Loveland (1986) studied a group of 5th grade SLD children and found that most children were LD in all three Rs, but that 18% had specific arithmetic problems. This suggests that specific MD (SMD) could be more common than specific RD, for which estimates are generally around 10%. It has also been suggested that SMD is more prevalent in children from lower socio-economic levels (O'Hare et al. 1991).

Differences in tests used to assess mathematics skills, and the cut-off points for categorising poor achievement as a "disorder" are likely to be responsible for the variations in prevalence estimates when comparing various studies. Such estimates can also be affected by the fact that it is often unclear when maths problems begin, so age at assessment may influence findings. Some children may make apparently normal progress in the first few years, especially if they have good rote memories and can master simple operations, but once demands become more complex their deficiencies in problem solving become evident.

It is also quite likely that there are children whose capacity for mathematics is below average without them having what might be presumed to be any kind of "disorder". All children have varying patterns of strengths and weaknesses in academic ares. Being relatively poor at maths may be a consequence of the individual cognitive profile of the child, in which some of the necessary skills for calculating are weak or require more effort than other kinds of learning. Children may react by turning away from, or "turning off" the learning of maths, by avoiding as much as possible, feeling uncomfortable and anxious about maths, and hence falling further behind their classmates. Whether this constitutes a "primary learning disorder" is debatable.

Nevertheless, there are children who do seem to have specific cognitive difficulties related to mathematics which can be identified through carefully targeted and thorough assessment. As Hughes (1986) in his book on children and the learning of mathematics notes, it is essential to try to diagnose exactly what processes are problematic for the individual child. He gives some vivid examples of variability among children in the different areas of mathematical understanding.

TYPES OF MATHEMATICAL DEFICITS

In his studies of adult patients with dyscalculia, Luria identified four types of problems:

a) *Deficits of logic* seen in problems with spatial order (such as understanding "the circle below the square"), or spatial memory, and also in writing lists of numbers with digits in the correct order, or dealing with calendars and clocks.

b) *Defects in planning*, or developing problem-solving strategies through the preliminary analysis of a problem. This is often needed in the kinds of problems presented to people such as: "a man is forty years old, his wife is ten years younger and his son's age is one third of his wife's age. How old is the boy?".

c) *Perseverating* with procedures that are not appropriate to new and different problems; or, inflexibility in application of problem-solving strategies (for example continuing to divide by 2, a strategy that had been learned to solve a previous problem but which was quite wrong for a new problem).

d) *Inability to do simple calculations*, for example not being able to use multiplication tables, or using inefficient counting or addition strategies when what was required was to multiply two figures. For example, when asked to multiply 3 by 3 the individual keeps on adding threes to the original one.

These specific syndromes have not been systematically studied in children although it has been claimed that Type (a) and Type (c) do exist, and certainly examples of the behaviours characteristic of each type can be observed in children having problems with arithmetic (Ginsberg, 1977).

Many researchers and educators in the mathematics field have tried to dissect mathematics into its various skills and components, and to trace the developmental learning pathway for young children as they move from practical knowledge of counting, which is present from early in life, to understanding of the signs, symbols, and processes that are fundamental to mathematics success. That is, they are "process" rather than pathology oriented. But despite books such as that of Hughes (1986), Fuson (1988), and others, there is not the abundance of literature in this field that is available for literacy development and disorders. We know quite a bit about how children begin to grasp basic mathematical processes from studies such as those of Hughes, but relatively little about how and why this kind of learning falters and becomes a problem for some children.

MATHEMATICAL PROCESSING

Many steps, rules, and facts are involved in even relatively simple arithmetic calculations and the child may have difficulties with any or all of the required processes. The kinds of problems that have been identified in children with maths problems are numerous. There are:

- problems with simple counting knowledge, and with ordination (first, second, third, etc.);
- failure to recognise arithmetical signs or symbols;
- difficulties in aligning numbers during addition, multiplication, etc.;
- failure to become competent in fundamental processes such as addition, subtraction, division etc.;
- extreme slowness in carrying out these operations (although given time, children with processing speed disadvantages may get there).

Slowness is sometimes associated with use of immature strategies such as counting on fingers, or counting aloud; this can make the process very inefficient. But it is important to distinguish between children who are slow and inefficient but who finally achieve solution, from those who truly lack basic computational skills.

Other problems may include not knowing procedures such as borrowing and carrying, not knowing where to place decimal points, and not understanding fractions. These deficiencies may underlie failure to be able to carry out complex written computation such as multi-digit multiplication.

Failure to make sense of symbols and symbolic relationships, to reason about common factors, to generate and apply verbal labelling strategies, to generalise or to reason by analogy with other procedures or problems, will also hinder learning of mathematics. These are conceptual and information-processing strategies which need to be applied to all kinds of learning not just mathematics, and which also form part of what we call intelligence.

Badian (1983) has also described a substantial sub-group of SMD children she calls an "attentional-sequential" group. These were children who knew *how* to do arithmetic but were often incorrect because they omitted a figure in a column, or forgot to carry a figure, failed to change operations when the sign changed, and had trouble recalling basic number facts such as multiplication tables. That is, they failed to focus adequate attention on the task and to make the necessary checks of the details of their work.

In a review of cognitive, neuropsychological, and genetic components of SMD, Geary (1993) provides summaries of experimental studies of arithmetic skills, which have identified specific problems and which suggest a way of constructing sub-types of MD children based on specific individual patterns of difficulties. It is clear that children whose counting strategies remain at a low level in the early years, or which are persistently insecure, will have ongoing difficulties across all areas of mathematics. Geary suggests that MD children have two basic numerical problems: immature arithmetical strategies with frequent procedural errors; and fundamental difficulties in the retrieval of arithmetic facts from long-term memory. Further, he sees the first problem as more of a *delay* in acquiring basic concepts, and the second as a more sustained *deficit*. Immature strategies, slow processing and solution achievement, together with computational and memory errors are characteristic of these children. Slow counting speed may contribute to problems in working memory because the material may decay before the end of the counting process is completed. This in turn will limit what goes into long-term memory.

Conceptualising the problems at a somewhat different cognitive and behavioural level, Munro (1986) describes children with maths problems as passive and disorganised learners who do not know how to go about dealing with mathematical ideas. They do not seem to know what to do with the instructions they are given. Such children often have to have repeated explanations of the same ideas; they do not perceive patterns and relationships that are obvious to the non-MD child; they find it hard to remember the steps in a procedure; they are unsure where to begin; they forget previously learned material; and they have difficulty comprehending instructions. Munro describes them as needing assistance focused on "how to learn" mathematics.

Children who find maths difficult or incomprehensible or hard to remember from one day to the next are highly likely to give up trying. They develop a picture of themselves as "no good at maths" and are hampered in further learning by their feelings of defeat. Hence anxiety over maths is likely to be a significant factor in continuing failure (Garnett & Fleishchner 1987).

Children with poor motivation or emotional disturbance may also be especially vulnerable to mathematics difficulties (Strang & Rourke, 1985).

ASSESSMENT OF SMD

Careful assessment of the exact nature of the problems is essential, including an analysis of the role of the child's reading skills and how they may impinge on mathematical learning, as well as some attention to the role of anxiety about mathematics learning.

Assessing number reading, writing, and recognition skills is an obvious first step. Children can also be asked to indicate the larger or smaller of two numbers to assess the understanding of the structure of the number system. Counting skills and counting strategies should be investigated, as exemplified in some of the screening test measures such as the Wide Range Achievement Test, written Arithmetic sub-test (see Chapter 4). Difficulties with spatial processing and organisation of numbers on the page may emerge when children are given written computation tasks.

As well as assessing their grasp of more mechanical functions, a major task in the diagnosis of these children is identifying the strategies they use (or fail to use) in approaching maths problems. What do they say to themselves as they set about problem solving? Do they perhaps not know how to plan and talk, or think, their way through the task? Self-instruction or verbalising techniques can help a child to construct the problem (e.g. "I need to break this problem down into smaller bits, to get started"). Children competent in mathematics can often articulate how they went about instructing themselves through the necessary computational and reasoning steps.

Compared with the availability of tests of many different aspects of reading, there are few well-normed comprehensive tests of mathematics. In the case example at the beginning of this chapter, a test called Key Math-Revised was used. This assessment tool (Connolly, 1988) is subtitled "A diagnostic inventory of essential mathematics". It includes tests of many of the basic processes noted throughout this chapter. It is also possible to obtain a teaching programme based on the same model. This useful test will be described in Chapter 4. Many educators develop their own assessment tools for classroom use and can use these to describe the difficulties in various areas of mathematics experienced by SMD children. Few of these "criterion-referenced" tests have published normative data to allow any age/grade objective comparisons which would underpin diagnosis of SMD, but they can be helpful for teachers in identifying specific weaknesses.

UNDERLYING DEFICITS IN SMD CHILDREN

Many kinds of deficits likely to be associated with SMD have been proposed including: auditory verbal deficits; visual spatial deficits, motor deficits, working memory problems, attention deficits, speed of processing problems, and social and emotional problems (Baker & Cantwell, 1985). Such a list suggests that there is great overlap of problems in any population of SLD children, no matter what their presenting learning difficulties, hence probing for specific underlying deficits may not be especially helpful in identifying a particular disorder. Like RD, SMD is a heterogeneous handicap, and is likely to have a variety of underlying cognitive impairments and of causal factors.

Despite this complexity, it is tempting to assume that some kind of probably quite subtle neurological dysfunction might be responsible for SMD in children. In part this assumption derives from the historical tradition of "discovering" impairments in adults who have sustained brain damage in particular parts of the brain that are associated with the loss of mathematical ability. Syndromes or collections of symptoms relating to types of difficulties have then been related to localised or specific sites of impairment in the brain such as the occipital, frontal, temporal, or parietal lobes, or some combination of these (see Luria, 1966, for examples). A more recent example comes from Grafman et al. (1989) who described the case of a Vietnam veteran whose left side of the brain was almost destroyed, with consequent loss of language skills. As this individual was still able to write numbers, recognise arithmetic symbols, and carry out simple computations, it was argued that the right side of the brain must play a role in at least some aspects of mathematical processing. The common belief that calculation and symbolic manipulation is predominantly a function of the left brain is challenged by findings in this case.

It is of interest to note that there has been at least one study of children with "acquired" SMD as a consequence of cortical lesions (Hecaen, 1976) which reported a high frequency of arithmetic difficulties associated with brain lesions. These appeared to be associated with lesions in the left hemisphere of the brain. It is also possible to find reported single case studies indicating the presence of left *and / or* right hemisphere involvement in children with arithmetic problems (e.g. Wilkening, 1984).

When considering childhood problems in this neuropsychological framework, however, there are a number of questions. First there is the documented association between mathematical and reading disabilities in a large proportion of SLD children, suggesting that if there is a neurological basis it is likely to take in a number of brain systems and areas. Second, mathematics, like language, is a system of symbols that represent relationships and convey ideas and concepts. So it is possible that impairments in "symbolic functions" might underlie both reading and mathematical problems. Third, numerous studies show that neurological impairment in and of itself does not necessarily lead to either general or specific cognitive disabilities in children. There is a myriad of other influences including early caretaking and family environmental factors, socioeconomic factors, teaching methods, and other developmental, psychological, and educational support factors that have powerful effects. It is extremely difficult in most cases of developmental disabilities to identify simple "brain–behaviour based" cause–effect relationships.

Fourth, most data on children with SMD come from studies of children where the cause of the difficulties is unknown and where there is no evidence of neurological or anatomical abnormalities. Hence we have no evidence on the cognitive/neurological connections in children which are relevant to SMD, and can only speculate on their existence, based to a limited extent on a few single-case, cognitive neuropsychological studies. It is most unusual to find any kind of specificity between brain lesion and type of mathematical deficit.

Clinical findings from adult neurology may be helpful in fractionating types of processes involved in mathematics, but we need the kind of model building and testing that has been so helpful in understanding RD over the last two decades, to be applied to SMD.

Nevertheless there is a continuing search for explanations of the problems for SLD children in mathematical areas, which are based on the theory that brain impairments of various kinds, as exemplified in performance on particular tests, may be related to specific cognitive difficulties (see Chapter 5). The evidence reviewed by Geary (1993) suggests commonalities in the findings from developmental and acquired "dyscalculias" (Temple, 1991; McCloskey, 1992) encompassing spatially based difficulties (which are right hemisphere based) as one category, reading and writing of numbers (which is left hemisphere based) as another; and "anarithmetica" or problems in recall of basic arithmetic facts (left hemisphere based) as the third.

SEARCHING FOR SUB-GROUPS OF SMD CHILDREN

As has been the case for RD, there have been attempts to identify sub-groups of SMD children who might differ in ways that would illuminate our understanding of mathematical difficulties.

One example of the cognitive profiling approach based on detailed assessment is a study by Strang and Rourke (1985), who studied three groups of SLD children. The first included children who were equally handicapped in reading, spelling, and arithmetic; the second group was much better at arithmetic than at reading and spelling, which were both similarly impaired; and the third group contained children whose reading and spelling were average or above but who had specific problems with arithmetic.

They identified several categories of difficulty in the specific arithmetic disabled group as follows:

- *Spatial organisation problems* (e.g. misalignment of numbers in columns and directionality problems (subtracting from left to right).
- *Procedural errors* such as missing an essential step in a problem.
- *Visual detail errors* such as misreading addition or subtraction signs.
- *Failure to change processes* or "set" (e.g. continuing to add when the sign has changed to minus).
- *Graphomotor problems* like illegible or reversed numbers.
- *Judgement and reasoning errors* such as attempting problems well beyond the child's capacity.

Rourke and his colleagues (see Rourke & Del Dotto, 1994) have also argued that some of the SMD children showed deficits in social competence, especially in recognising and interpreting feeling and motivations in other people. However, although some of these results appear to have been supported by other researchers in North America and in Europe, the connections between social and emotional deficits, and specific difficulties with mathematics are hard to interpret and still require more research.

There were varying patterns of neurocognitive abilities as demonstrated on test performance of children from the differing sub-groups. On the basis of these patterns, Strang and Rourke (1985) argued that the SMD group had problems with processing subserved by the right hemisphere of the brain, whereas the children with spelling and reading problems, but *not* arithmetic problems, were weak in processes served by the left hemisphere.

However, as Strang and Rourke point out, there are so many complex steps and functions involved in calculation that it is hard to see how such diverse processes could all be located in one side of the brain. Furthermore, given that the left side of the brain is more proficient at processing symbolic/abstract and temporally ordered or sequential material, it is unlikely that it would not be involved in mathematics processes which are both symbolic and sequential in many ways. Again this emphasises the speculative nature of presumptions of connections between MD and brain dysfunction.

In another attempt at searching for specific underlying factors in sub-groups, Siegel and Linder (1984) compared reading *and* arithmetic disabled children, those with normal reading but arithmetic difficulties, and normally achieving children, on several short-term memory tasks. Although all LD children were poorer than normal children on the tasks, it was of interest that the purely MD children were rather less disadvantaged in remembering auditory as compared with visual stimuli. This finding is consistent with that of Strang and Rourke (1985) whose SMD group was notably poorer than the other group in visual-perceptual and visual-spatial abilities, and much better on auditory-perceptual tasks. These children also had a higher verbal than performance IQ. Fletcher and Loveland (1986) reported similar results indicating poorer performance on non-verbal tasks in their SMD samples alongside strengths in verbal recall. Together these results offer some support for the contribution of more specific deficits in visual–spatial processes in this group.

However Ceci and Peters (1980) have cautioned that perceptual skills are a complex of many different components and that the SMD children in their research had little difficulty with most of the auditory and visual factors they tested. Trying to remediate MD with "popular" programmes aimed at building visual-perceptual skills may be neither theoretically nor practically useful.

Share, Moffitt, and Silva (1988) compared 11-year-old children from a New Zealand community sample who had either a specific arithmetic disorder or who had both reading and arithmetic problems. They found that children with *both* sets of problems were significantly impaired on language-based or left hemisphere tasks, but less so on non-language-based tasks. *Boys* with SMD showed the reverse pattern of less impairment on language/left hemisphere tasks, while their non-verbal skills were poorer than those of non-disabled comparison children. However girls with specific arithmetic disability could not be differentiated from controls on any of the measures. Such findings suggest: (a) the need to be cautious in speculating about brain hemispheric influences on SMD and (b), the need to consider boys and girls separately in studies of SLD, as they may arrive at the same end point by different pathways. Much of the data in this field comes from studies of clinic-referred boys only; these cases may not be typical of SMD children as a group. Hence studies of community samples of carefully defined sub-groups are particularly useful in understanding the way SMD presents amongst a "normal" population of school-aged children.

Other researchers have not been able to identify neuropsychological differences between specific arithmetic disabled and comparison non-disabled children, matched for reading level. This area awaits more sophisticated research in which clearly differentiated groups of SLD children can be compared on tests that are validated measures of particular brain functions. Such research is still very much in its infancy and is handicapped by limitations in knowledge of brain–behaviour relationships particularly during the developmental period. Assumptions that particular functions including those involved in mathematics can be pinpointed in particular brain areas should be viewed with caution.

Luria (1980) for example, has suggested that no particular site in the brain is responsible for any complex function. Behaviour such as solving mathematical problems will involve coordination of many brain areas. In addition, complex processing of information, including maths problems may be achieved by a variety of different ways depending on the capacities, cognitive styles, and strategies of the particular individual, and the way the problems are presented. As we are dealing with *developmental disabilities*, the changes in brain development and function involved in skill learning over time must be taken into account. For example, the qualitative and quantitative differences between early learning stages, involving perhaps slow and laborious processing, and the overlearned, smoothly operating routines that will become available to the learner in time, must impinge on the ways in which the brain functions in dealing with mathematical challenges. It should not be surprising that developmental disabilities may be different in expression and origin from acquired disabilities. Our relatively limited knowledge of SMD suggests that more emphasis is needed on this aspect of the broader field of SLD, whether SMD is studied as a specific problem, or in combination with reading and spelling difficulties.

We have little knowledge about the long-term outcome for children with SMD. There are reports of chronic difficulties continuing into adulthood and also of cases where problems are overcome (Baker & Cantwell, 1985). It is unknown how outcome relates to the nature or severity of SMD, to its association with other learning problems, or to other educational or psychosocial factors. Nor do we have systematic data concerning the effect of remedial interventions with SMD children, or which methods have greater efficacy in the general teaching of mathematics in the classroom. Trial and error approaches to remediation are the most common, although many workers stress the importance of teaching problem-solving strategies. Older literature suggesting that perceptual-motor training was useful for SMD is not supported by evaluation research.

SUMMARY

SMD has not been clearly defined using agreed criteria but it is likely that it affects a substantial number of children, and can occur in combination with other SLDs or as a single area of deficit. In contrast with the voluminous literature on reading difficulties, there is little research on SMD and this area of understanding has apparently suffered from relative neglect in the psychological if not the educational field. This may be because numeracy problems are considered less of a handicap in the community by comparison with reading problems. Neuropsychological theory is underdeveloped at this point in time, although it has been argued (Geary, 1993) that there is some convergence between knowledge of the development of arithmetical skill, and the descriptions of deficits in "acquired" cases of MD. Tentative suggestions which might provide useful avenues for further research can be made, however. There is some indication that visual memory processing problems may be implicated in SMD; these may underpin difficulties in recognising and remembering symbols such as subtract, divide, decimals etc., in the early learning stages; and spatial order and spatial memory, in more complex tasks. Strategy deficits are so common in SMD children that they must be a key focus for teaching and remediation theory and practice. Their role in mathematical processing problems is almost certainly a general rather than a specific one. Many of the identified deficits such as verbal memory, understanding of symbols, and sequential ordering, are key elements in literacy as well as numeracy problems and may be primary characteristics of children with difficulties in reading, spelling, and mathematics. They can be tentatively related to left hemisphere processing weaknesses. Claims that social/emotional problems are characteristic of SMD children require further investigation. They may play a causal role; they may be a consequence of failure and loss of confidence; they may be a function of which children are identified as having maths difficulties; or they may be chance associations.

This chapter has produced more questions than answers about SMD, hence the repeated pleas for more research to increase our understanding.

CHAPTER FOUR

Diagnosis and assessment: Methods and measures

The aims of clinical, psychological, and educational assessment of an SLD child are:

- to achieve understanding of the learning problems as seen by all the major individuals involved with the child and of course the child himself or herself;
- to understand the history of the problem;
- to assess the specific nature of the child's SLDs and his or her cognitive and behavioural strengths and weaknesses;
- to arrive at a formulation of the problem which leads to recommendations or prescriptions for the provision of well-targeted assistance for the child, and suggests how teachers or parents may help.

Before outlining methods and measures used in assessing and diagnosing SLD, it is important to look at the preliminary steps in any referral and assessment process.

Children are usually referred for assessment by parents or teachers who are concerned that the child is not doing well at school. They are puzzled and uncertain about why this should be so. They wonder if the child is intellectually disabled, has vision or hearing problems, is "lazy", or preoccupied with some personal troubles, is bored because the work is not at a suitable level, or has some other obscure problems. Not uncommonly a child will have difficulties in maintaining attention to the teacher, or to the current classroom activity, or to his or her assigned work, and may be a disruptive and distracting influence. This will also be a source of frustration and concern to teachers and often to parents.

HEALTH PROBLEMS

Children who are struggling with reading will sometimes have had their eyes tested and possibly their hearing, because these seem the most obvious possible handicaps that could underlie the problem. If this has not been done, and there are signs of visual discomfort, such as the child complaining that he or she cannot see the blackboard or the letters on the page clearly, then it may need to be attended to in the early stages of assessment. But it is important to reiterate that *visual problems do not cause SLDs*, despite some popular beliefs to the contrary. Hearing and language impairments in the early development of the child, however, can often play a role as risk factors for SLDs.

Although most SLD children do not have complicating medical conditions (indeed these are excluded by most definitions of SLDs), problems in learning can be associated with a variety of developmental and health complications. Perhaps the most common of these, is a history of otitis media, or "glue ear". This is a condition that is relatively common in early childhood where the child has a recurring infection which affects the ear, nose, and throat. The middle ear becomes infected, and this can "glue up" hearing so that the child either misses much of the auditory information around him or her or hears it imperfectly through a sort of fog. Some children have many episodes of otitis media and this can mean that they miss out on a good deal of information in the classroom, in a cumulating way over time. Such difficulties can have the secondary effect of causing a child to "switch off" from his or her classroom surroundings because so much effort is required to focus on auditory messages. This can put such children at risk for learning delays and serious gaps in their knowledge.

Other behaviours that may be observed or reported in the child which suggest the need for investigation include: poor speech articulation; slurred or unintelligible speech; frequent rubbing of eyes; bumping into people or objects constantly; impaired ability to handle materials such as pencils, scissors etc., i.e. problems in gross and fine motor control; "absences"—when the child may stare into space for a few moments and appear to be out of contact, which may suggest a mild form of epilepsy; frequent and very intense outbursts of rage or distress; and difficulties in remembering and following instructions. Referral to a paediatrician, speech therapist, audiologist, occupational therapist, eye specialist etc. may be indicated in a proportion of cases of children who are not learning at a normal rate and who show such "neurodevelopmental" symptoms.

Although it is safe to say that only a minority of SLD children have a history of health problems, it is clearly important to check on this aspect of a referred child's development.

REFERRAL PROCEDURES

The child and his or her teachers and parents approach the assessment with their own set of expectations, anxieties, and attitudes. These are influential in what follows. For example, the child who is hostile, resistant and who comes to the assessment against his or her will cannot be properly assessed while that resistance remains. Parents sometimes have difficulty telling the child why he or she is being brought for assessment, and may explain nothing about it at all, or offer spurious reasons, so that the child is puzzled and anxious about the pending meeting. Some children believe they are going to "the doctor" because they might have a mysterious disorder, or are being checked out for bad behaviour, or are going to take a "test". It is essential that the child has a clear idea of what the visit is about. Parents or teachers, or other referring professionals who may have the task of communicating what is to happen, can explain that they are worried about the difficulties with school work, and are looking for expert help to see whether there are any problems that could be remedied to help the child feel more comfortable and confident about learning.

The assessment should not be presented as a threat, or an inquisition, or "exams", or tests, which will put the child in an anxiety-provoking situation; but as an attempt to analyse something that is worrying everyone. It should be explained that many children have some difficulties at school and that it is normal and sensible to go and see someone about it, just as one does when there are problems with physical health.

Younger children sometimes think they might be going to get an injection, or will be medically treated in some way. Careful explanations of the procedures to be expected, and answers to the child's questions are essential before the first visit. Providing an estimate of the time involved in the assessment process is also helpful for parent and child.

Parents and teachers can sometimes also approach assessment defensively. The parent who comes with an agenda involving conflict with the school such as rejection, or dissatisfaction with advice from school personnel, or seeking an agent who will support the parent in a battle to control the child or to have the child "work harder" is unlikely to give an objective account of the presenting problems. Such a parent is also likely to have transmitted that special agenda to the child, even if in subtle form. Some children are afraid to give their own opinions and insights into the problem, or to express their concerns or resentments, for fear of conflict with what they perceive might be important to the parent.

Teachers who feel that their competence is being judged may also have difficulty being objective about the problems when they are asked for an opinion.

Some parents have deep-seated but unexpressed fears that the child might be retarded, or that their own behaviour has in some way "caused" the learning problems, or that their child is going to be like some other member of the family, who failed at school and was not a success in life. The clinician needs to be very sensitive to all these dynamics, and to take account of them in arriving at a formulation of the problem. Both the expressed and unexpressed, or more subtle, attitudes that child and caretakers bring to the assessment form a very valuable part of the data. As they may take some time to emerge clearly in a coherent and comprehensible way during a series of interviews, it is ill-advised to look for a "quick fix" single-session assessment which does not permit the development of in-depth knowledge of the child's background.

Similarly, it is essential to put together information from as many informed sources as possible in seeking to understand why things have gone wrong for this child.

The first step in assessment, then, involves taking a detailed history of the problems, and other relevant aspects of the child's development, and integrating this with accounts of the learning difficulties given by the child, the parents, and the school.

TAKING A HISTORY

This includes a number of basic steps and questions:

1. Obtain from the parents a summary of the child's developmental history including such issues as: was this a planned pregnancy; were the pregnancy and birth normal or abnormal; were there any early childhood problems such as frequent illness, failure to thrive, delayed milestones such as sitting, walking, talking, and toilet training.

At what age did language develop and were there any problems with articulation, comprehension etc?

How did the child adapt to siblings, other children, relatives?

Were there any events such as hospitalisation, accidents, or injuries to the child, or family illnesses or deaths, which might have set back the child's development?

Description of early adjustment to kindergarten and school is essential.

Did the child show problems with focusing on tasks, paying attention, hearing and understanding instructions, sitting still and listening to stories?

What are current relationships with teachers, peers, and family members like? What kind of temperament does the child have; has he or she been easy or difficult to get along with?

This gathering of a developmental history will give a picture of the child and his or her environment and how he or she has adapted to developmental challenges. It will also be critical in understanding the background of the child and the context for the development of school difficulties. This developmental history information has to be taken into account in planning the assessment procedures, and later, in guiding the nature of recommendations for intervention. For example, a history of delayed milestones, including language development, already provides some hypotheses about the origins of the difficulties which need to be tested out in the assessment procedures.

2.   Obtain a clear and detailed description of the presenting problems. The parent's and child's view of the current difficulties and how they arose, the intervention strategies that have been tried in the past, their own analysis and explanation of the difficulties, their hopes for the future and their expectations of the child, need to be covered. If there have been previous assessments, copies of such assessments should be seen if possible, as their details and conclusions may provide important background information. Are there are other family members who have had difficulties with learning, or with psychosocial adjustment? This is particularly relevant for reading and spelling difficulties which have a tendency to be present in more than one family member. A positive family history for cognitive problems suggests at least some genetic influence which can contribute to understanding why the child may have learning problems.

LIAISING WITH THE SCHOOL

Obtaining a comprehensive report from the school concerning the child's particular learning problems, his or her behavioural adjustment inside and outside the classroom, his or her strengths and weaknesses, an account of previous attempts to help that have been tried (if any), and the teacher's own views of the child and the learning difficulties, is extremely important. This liaison will need to be done with parental consent; where this is withheld, thus prohibiting consultation with the class teacher, it represents a severe limitation on the adequacy of the assessment and on the understanding and formulation of the case.

Gathering school-based information is best done in a structured manner. That is, whether personal face-to-face, phone, or written contact is made, there should be a systematic format to the enquiries rather than a general non-specific request for information which leaves it up to the teacher to provide whatever comes to mind. Structured or systematic information may be achieved in various ways: via a questionnaire covering all facets of school behaviour which the teacher may complete and return by mail (and in confidence); via an equally structured phone or face-to-face interview which in addition to providing the same kind of information as the questionnaire, allows scope for the teacher to express insights, opinions, anecdotes, examples etc. which are often very valuable; or via a letter to the school in which the areas of information being sought are specified, including the nature of the particular learning disabilities, and classroom behaviour, along with a request to cover all specified aspects as fully as possible.

Past school reports can be a useful source of data and should always be requested. However they can also be rather bland and unenlightening, as many schools do not wish to put negative comments on childrens' reports and will try to emphasise the positive aspects of the child's progress. Alternatively they can occasionally be too judgemental, such as in calling a child "lazy", or not trying hard enough, and this is not very helpful in understanding the nature of the child's difficulties. Children are not normally lazy in the face of learning experiences, (just watch them working to achieve mastery in non-threatening situations); if they appear so it is probably because they are bored, feel helpless, angry, or anxious and afraid of failure.

It is often the case that observation of the child in the school setting is desirable to enrich the picture that is developing and at the same time, face-to-face consultation with the teacher is usually illuminating. He or she will be able to estimate where the child is performing in relation to other peers in the same curriculum, the specific situations that are creating difficulties, the general behavioural adjustment of the child, and the kinds of assistance that have been offered previously and how effective they have been. Classroom observation is not a simple matter, as the act of observation introduces the risk of lack of naturalness or normalcy to the situation. Teacher, child, and classmates may behave differently when they know they are being watched. There is no easy solution to this problem although the observer should remain as unobtrusive as possible. Notwithstanding the artificiality of the situation, valuable information can be gained about the child's behaviour in class, how well-controlled and self-regulated he or she is, how he or she interacts with the teacher, the conditions of the classroom in which the child works, his or her ability to focus on assigned work, to attend to spoken and written material being presented by the teacher, and the child's interactions with peers. A school visit also provides a valuable opportunity to talk with members of staff who have concerns about the child.

THE CHILD'S INTRODUCTION

Before commencing an assessment it is preferable to spend time "chatting" to the child about school, teachers, friends, favourite activities, sport, TV etc; in fact any topic that will engage interest. This should be "low key" not inquisitorial, and should follow any lines suggested by the child's responses. If the child wishes to complain angrily, or sadly, about the hard time he or she is having, this is also legitimate and often very helpful in leading to an understanding of the child's view of the situation.

Some children will deny or minimise the difficulties; some will be most unforthcoming with monosyllabic responses and apparent lack of cooperation. A child may say little for a variety of reasons:

a) he or she may have poor language skills and find verbal interaction especially with strangers, very difficult;

b) he or she may be very shy, or need a long time to begin to interact comfortably with a new acquaintance;

c) he or she may be resentful, angry, hostile, or depressed, at having been brought out of school or to a strange place, or to be missing out on a preferred activity (so it is preferable not to arrange assessment to conflict with the child's favourite sports lesson for example);

d) he or she may feel very threatened and defensive by the whole procedure.

Time, and a sensitive, warm and positive atmosphere will usually help the child to begin to trust the clinician, but it is not a process that can be rushed through. It is helpful to assess in a comfortable and casually arranged room which looks more like a family room than a "surgery", and which contains pictures and objects related to children's interests.

ILLUSTRATIVE CASE HISTORY

Peter was 9½ and in Grade 4 when he was referred to the clinic for assessment because he was struggling with reading, writing, and spelling. During the first interview Peter's mother reported a normal pregnancy and delivery and that Peter's early development showed no areas of concern. He walked at about 12 months and began to say his first words about the same time. He was toilet trained by the age of 2. Although he had no eating and sleeping difficulties as a young child, at the time of the assessment his mother reported that he was a "fussy" eater and he required one of his parents to stay with him until he fell asleep at night. He had also been bedwetting intermittently since he went to school, and his mother reported that this could be triggered by events at school such as being bullied. Peter had had no serious illnesses or injuries and all milestones appear to have been in the normal range.

According to his parents, Peter's literacy problems were apparent by the latter half of Grade 2. However his progress in maths has been good unless he is faced with language-based problems (e.g. a boy had two apples which cost 10 cents each etc.). It was reported that Peter had poor word attack skills, problems in pronouncing some syllables, and with triple blends (e.g. "spr"); he had difficulty writing sentences and occasionally reversed letters. The school had provided some remedial assistance but Peter still failed to achieve normal levels of literacy. He did not like school, and his parents had difficulty persuading him to get ready in the mornings. He avoided reading whenever he could.

The teacher report described Peter as a shy, serious child who was sensitive to criticism, lacking in motivation and enthusiasm, and with problems in completing set tasks. His expressive and receptive language skills were weak, and he had trouble telling the time. She noted that his strengths were his general knowledge, his arithmetic ability, and his sense of humour.

Assessment

Although Peter appeared very anxious about being tested, and worried about making errors, he worked consistently and tried hard. His attention span was adequate but he seemed somewhat depressed about himself and his experiences with schoolwork. He was very responsive to praise and was keen to please the tester. He spoke in short single sentences, sometimes showing word-finding difficulties, and he was not able to elaborate on his brief answers. His intellectual ability as assessed with the Wechsler Intelligence Scale for Children–Version III, was in the average range with greatest strengths in Mental Arithmetic and Concept Identification, and on performance tests including Block Design and Picture Arrangement. His weakest areas were in Vocabulary, that is, the ability to supply word definitions, and in the Information sub-test which assesses learned information.

On the Neale Analysis of Reading Ability–Revised, Peter's reading level was only at an age equivalent level of $7\frac{1}{2}$ years on accuracy of word recognition, and slightly lower on comprehension, thus confirming his serious delay (two years) in reading skills. Most of his errors in reading were word substitutions—he guessed at words he did not know (e.g. started instead of sheltered), rather than trying to sound them out. He did not know the sounds of a number of letters, and could not segment the sounds of longer words such as "umbrella". His spelling was at a Grade 2 level and here again he guessed the spelling based on a few letters, often leaving letters out and getting them in the wrong order (e.g. he wrote "enet" for "enter").

Because of the concerns with Peter's limitations in language skills, he was given some sub-tests of the Illinois Test of Psycholinguistic Abilities. Verbal Expression, Auditory Closure, and Sound Blending skills were all at least two years behind age-appropriate level. Peter was able to print his name and to copy shapes but could only write two brief sentences when asked to write a short piece about something he had done recently. His fear of not being able to spell words he wanted for his story seemed to inhibit him from producing any more material.

In this assessment there was clear evidence of severe limitations in phonological skills which could be applied to word analysis for reading and spelling. Hence, an intensive phonologically based, daily reading remediation programme was recommended for Peter, along with integrated language work involving greater emphasis on expressing himself verbally, and plenty of encouragement and praise for any attempts at speaking, reading, and writing. Modification of the amount and type of homework he was expected to do, with provision of visual cues as part of the homework instructions was also suggested.

In order to attend to Peter's anxiety and resistance to going to school, it was also suggested that he be given further behavioural assessment and treatment so that the cycle of avoidance behaviour which might adversely affect success with a remedial programme would be reduced. A school visit was arranged to see if Peter's avoidant behaviour had any basis in his classroom and playground experiences. His parents, who were highly motivated to help, were given advice on how to go about helping Peter with a small amount of reading and spelling practice each night in ways that would maximize his feelings that he was making progress.

ESSENTIALS OF ASSESSMENT

It is not too strong a claim to suggest that assessment and diagnosis of the SLD child's difficulties in the most detailed and accurate way is the most important and worthwhile step that can be taken along the way to intervention and improvement. A multidisciplinary approach with paediatrician, psychologist, and educator combining their skills in assessment of various aspects of the child's development is ideal.

In general, psychoeducational assessment must cover at least the six main factors of intelligence: academic achievement, language abilities, attention and memory, visual–spatial, and motor speed capacities. The psychometric part of the assessment covers a number of steps and procedures which should proceed in a logical order, taking into account the child's feelings and capacities to deal with assessment at every point. The younger the child, the shorter his or her concentration span, and ability to apply him or herself to the tasks over a prolonged period. Therefore test sessions should be carefully planned and monitored to make sure that the child is able to give of his or her best throughout.

Test validity requires that the estimates of abilities gained through testing represent the best the child is capable of, rather than what the child might give on any particular "off" day, or when he or she is feeling miserable, threatened, or anxious. So the development of rapport and a good working relationship is essential to begin with, and the assessor, whether teacher, paediatrician, psychologist, or other health professional will need to spend sufficient time to make sure that the child is as comfortable and motivated as possible.

Even though most tests are designed to be administered in a single session, it will often be necessary to take breaks within testing sessions, to give younger children especially, a chance to refocus their energies and attention after a short rest. This is particularly the case for very young children and for those who have serious attention and concentration problems.

Any adverse conditions or problems (e.g. the child seems very tired) during testing should be noted and allowed for, in arriving at the final formulation.

It is usually impossible to achieve a basic screening assessment covering intellectual abilities and academic measures in less than two sessions of at least one hour each. Follow-up assessments of specific language and cognitive functions may be recommended to enhance understanding of the specific difficulties that underlie the SLD, and to contribute to well-targeted recommendations for help.

The tests discussed here are a limited selection from a wide variety of available tools. They have been included as examples of useful ways of going about assessing children referred for learning problems, and are not intended to be the mandated set of tests. When working with children from different countries, language, and cultural background, it is necessary to give careful consideration to what are the best tools for assessment in those particular conditions. The assessment area is dominated by standardised tests developed in the USA, many of which have been translated into different languages, and for which national norms may be available. But extrapolation from expected or standardised scores in one culture to those in another must always be viewed with caution. For example, grade equivalent scores which can be obtained through some of the tests may vary in their meaning because children begin school at different ages in different countries.

STEPS IN THE ASSESSMENT

1. Basic screening tests

It is best to begin with a test of intelligence and problem-solving abilities so that the capacities of the child for academic learning can be estimated. *Exact* prediction of learning capacity on the basis of the Intelligence Quotient (IQ) as derived from such tests is not possible, but there is a strong association between IQ and academic success, hence this can be a useful guide to intellectual and academic potential. Perhaps more importantly, a good basic IQ test will show up areas where the child is having difficulties and where he or she is strong and confident, and it can provide considerable qualitative information about how a child goes about thinking and reasoning. For example, some children are impulsive guessers, some cannot bear to concede that they do not know the answer; others are extremely reluctant to guess at an answer and may not respond unless they feel certain they know. There is usually nothing particularly abnormal about these indications of "style"; they are part of individual differences amongst children, but they can give insights into why a child is inefficient in picking up information in the classroom.

The Wechsler Scales.   The most widely used test for assessment of overall cognitive abilities is probably the Wechsler Intelligence Scale for Children (WISC). There have been several updatings of this comprehensive IQ test, the latest being the WISC-III published in 1992. It has also been translated and adapted for use in a number of non-English speaking countries. This test contains 10 sub-tests which when summed together give an overall IQ with the mean for the population being 100 and the standard deviation being 15. There are also three supplementary tests to provide further information if required.

To be considered for a diagnosis of specific LD, it is usual that the overall IQ estimate should be at least 80, that is, not more than 20 points below average for the age level.

Within the WISC there are two groups of tests called Verbal and Performance tests. Verbal tests assess vocabulary knowledge (the child is asked to define words of increasing difficulty); comprehension of social conventions (e.g. why do we drive on the left-hand side of the road?); the ability to form functional and abstract concepts (in what way are an orange and a banana alike?); to do mental arithmetic; and to demonstrate knowledge of general information (e.g. the names of the four seasons of the year). There is also a supplementary test which asks the child to repeat from memory a series of digits, some forwards and some backwards. This is a simple auditory memory test which is particularly useful to include for children suspected of having SLDs.

The Performance tests assess the ability to pick out essential missing details from a picture, to analyse and synthesise patterns made from red and white blocks; the ability to put together jigsaw pieces to construct an object; the capacity for rapid transcribing of coded signs, and the ability to sequentially organise a series of sketched drawings so that they make a sensible story.

Looking at the pattern of abilities across these different aspects of problem solving, and across verbal and visuo-spatial reasoning tasks provides a profile of the child's abilities. It is not uncommonly found, for example, that RD children will have higher scores on the Performance, as compared to the Verbal scale. Some SLD children have difficulty with the particular sub-tests that tap "freedom from distraction" capacities, i.e. require the child to concentrate hard for a short period in processing and remembering what to do with new information in novel ways, such as in solving mental arithmetic problems.

The WISC is an attractive, challenging, and engaging test and most children enjoy working with it, if the atmosphere is congenial. It is almost certainly the test of first choice in assessing children suspected of having SLDs.

However it is not the best test for very young children, as although it has been standardised for children from the age of 6 to 16 years, it tends to overestimate IQ at the very youngest ages; furthermore it may not have enough scope or extended range for very bright adolescents.

The Stanford Binet. An alternative, highly respected and well standardised test is the Stanford Binet, now in its fourth edition. This has the advantage of starting at the age of 2 years and going right through into adulthood with sub-tests covering each age level. The latest edition of the Stanford Binet comprises sub-scales which fractionate intelligence into four areas: Verbal Reasoning, Abstract/Visual Reasoning, Quantitative Reasoning, and Short-term Memory. Putting together scores in these areas produces an overall test composite or IQ score as well as an informative profile across the domains.

The Verbal Reasoning scale includes vocabulary knowledge, recognising absurdities in pictured stimuli, recognising relationships between word classes, and comprehension of social, economic, survival, and political issues.

The Quantitative scale consists of 40 problems which cover a wide range of concepts related to mathematical knowledge and reasoning, and which are tested via block and picture tasks, as well as spoken word problems.

Tests of Abstract/Visual reasoning involve copying, pattern and design analysis and synthesis, and paper folding and cutting, i.e. visual performance tests, similar in concept to some of those in the WISC-III. Short-term Memory tests include memory for bead patterns, for spoken sentences, for digit strings (forwards and backwards), and for objects pictured on cards.

This most recent edition of the Stanford Binet provides profiles of strength and weakness across the various sub-tests and ability factors, which like the WISC factor profiles are very valuable in developing a discriminating picture of a child's abilities. This can then lead to hypothesis testing concerning the sources of difficulty in learning for an individual child.

For children who have been previously tested with the WISC, it may be advisable to choose the Stanford Binet to avoid test practice effects.

The British Ability Scales (BAS).   The BAS which was developed by British experts (Elliot, Murray, & Pearson, 1983), contains a comprehensive set of 23 scales measuring a range of cognitive abilities that cover the age range 2:5 to 17:5 years. Each of the scales can be used on its own for specific hypothesis-testing purposes, as well as in combination with other scales, and short forms are provided for most scales. A recent revision and standardisation of this test for use in the USA is called the Differential Ability Scales (DAS).

The BAS covers six process areas: speed of information processing (which is of course relevant across all cognitive domains); reasoning (which includes sub-tests of similarities, formal operational thinking, matrices, and social reasoning); spatial reasoning (including block design, letter rotation); perceptual matching (copying and letter matching); short-term memory (for designs, digits, and picture recognition); and retrieval and application of knowledge (including basic number and arithmetic skills, naming vocabulary, verbal comprehension and fluency, word definitions, word reading, and Piagetian conservation items). The BAS thus combines elements of school learning and performance, fluid and crystallised intelligence, and some neuropsychological components such as speed of information processing, visuo-spatial, and memory tasks. Combinations of scores from certain scales may be used to give an IQ score. However the strength of this test is very much in the comprehensive *profile* of abilities it can provide. Many of the sub-tests are similar in focus and content to some of the WISC tests. The arithmetic and number skills sub-tests can be used to obtain an assessment of numeracy problems; while the verbal and reading tests provide an assessment of literacy levels.

The authors provide some case material at the end of the Introductory Manual which is helpful in illustrating the uses and interpretations of BAS assessment with children with specific learning difficulties.

There are many other useful and attractive tests for young children which may be used as alternatives to the WISC, Stanford Binet, or BAS depending on individual needs and situations. These include the McCarthy Scales for children 2½ to 8½ years, which have sub-scales measuring verbal, perceptual/performance, memory, quantitative, and motor abilities, and from which an overall General Cognitive Index can be derived. It too is an engaging test which provides useful specific information especially for young children with learning problems.

The Columbia Mental Maturity Scale, a test of reasoning ability for children from 3½ to 10 years, is useful for very young children especially if they have verbal or physical difficulties that make the use of the WISC or the Stanford Binet inadvisable. This test requires no verbal communication, but a simple pointing response. The Leiter International Performance Scale is also a non-verbal test and is therefore useful for children with hearing or language problems. However these scales do not have the wealth of research and clinical data to substantiate their reliability and validity by comparison with the major instruments, and the Leiter at least, is somewhat out of date.

Further details on the tests noted here as well as reviews of a number of additional measures are available in Sattler (1992).

2. Targeting the referral question

Once a profile of abilities has been obtained, it is time to move on to assessment of reading, spelling, writing, and arithmetic, with the choice of the next measure being a function of the specific concerns about the learning problems of the particular child. If the problem seems to be concentrated on reading, for example, it may not be necessary at this preliminary stage to oblige the child to take a test of arithmetic. For some children who are presenting with obvious comprehension or expressive language difficulties, or for those whose test performance shows that they have more serious language impairments, referral to a speech therapist for a detailed language assessment is highly desirable.

Reading and Spelling.   Teachers in the classroom are able to administer a number of available reading and spelling tests which are graded across the primary school years, and which have been designed to suit the educational curricula and expected standards for a particular population, culture, and language. Many of these give estimates of word knowledge and comprehension using a multiple choice format for answers which shows where the child is by comparison with others at his or her age/grade level. Such tests vary from country to country and it is best to choose one that has sound psychometric properties and which is standardised for the community in which the child is being educated.

A very useful test for more detailed diagnostic purposes is the Neale Analysis of Reading Ability (Revised Edition, Neale, 1988). The child is asked to read aloud a short story; the number and types of errors are noted; errors or unknown words are corrected or supplied by the tester; and then the child is asked some comprehension questions for each passage. This test gives an age level and a standard score for reading rate, accuracy, and comprehension. These differentiated measures are extremely useful in considering variability in facets of reading skills. Some children, for example, can recognise many words in a parrot fashion but comprehend very little of the story; others are inaccurate in producing the words but are able to extract enough information despite their word recognition problems to comprehend reasonably well.

The Neale also has some diagnostic tests which can be used as follow-up for those children who do very poorly. These include auditory discrimination, spelling, and letter knowledge. There are two parallel forms of the test which means that after some remedial intervention a child may be retested on the alternate form to see whether he or she has made any progress. Careful recording of the errors made by the child in reading aloud permits the assessor to judge which strategies the child is using to help him or her to read. For example, pronunciation errors suggest that the child is trying to use some phonological skills which help in sounding out a new word, even though the child's print to sound translation is not very accurate. A predominance of visual (word substitution) errors, i.e. when the child guesses new words on the basis of letters they have in common with words he or she may know most of the time (see Peter's case history), suggests that the child is relying on "look say", or visual guess methods and may not have phonological strategies available.

Having a child read aloud lists of regular and irregular words is also useful in showing which strategies the child has available to tackle single words. The child who reads predominantly using phonological, sounding-out strategies will do better with regular words, and will struggle with irregular words. Children whose main strategy is direct visual word recognition should not show such differences, as they fail to apply phonological strategies which are very helpful with regular words (see Castles & Coltheart, 1993, for examples).

Other reading tests include the Standard Reading Tests of Daniels and Diack (1958), which is especially useful when a child is thought to be at the very beginning stage of reading and tests such as the Neale are too difficult. This test provides a reading age and grade standard, has word reading and recognition sub-tests, and a number of diagnostic tests for follow-up of children with problems on the basic reading measures. The sub-tests include copying abstract figures, copying a sentence, letter recognition, aural discrimination, spelling, and picture-word recognition. Little is known concerning the validity and reliability of this test which is now quite old, and it is most useful to provide qualitative information about the cognitive and pre-reading capacities of the individual, rather than being a well-standardised measure.

The Wide Range Achievement Test (Revised) (WRAT-III) and the Peabody Individual Achievement Tests (PIAT), are American normed omnibus tests which provide screening assessment of the three Rs. The WRAT, which covers the age range 5 years to adulthood, is particularly useful as an initial screening measure for LDs as it assesses single word reading, written spelling, and written arithmetic in individual assessment, in the one test which can be completed in not much more than half an hour. Learning problems identified through this screening can then be followed up with more detailed assessment by using more focused and comprehensive tests of each skill.

The advantage of the PIAT is that it is uses many multiple choice tests for some of which the child just has to point at the correct answer. Hence it can be useful for language-handicapped or very anxious children who find a pointing response less intimidating than having to actually produce something. The sub-tests included in the PIAT are mathematics, reading recognition, reading comprehension, spelling, and general information. It covers the age range from the beginning to the end of school. It is useful for ascertaining a child's general level of achievement by comparison with same-aged children (albeit only with US children's data).

Other widely used (US-based) tests of academic areas are the Woodcock-Johnson Psycho-Educational Battery–Revised, and the Kaufman Test of Educational Achievement. All of these tests give profiles of educational achievement across the key areas and can be used as summaries of a child's levels, and/or as a jumping-off point for more detailed exploration of problem areas. Most countries have a range of tests of the three Rs which are appropriate for their own population and language; some can be used by teachers, others are restricted to psychologists. It is clearly beyond the scope of this chapter to review and evaluate all of these tests. Their purposes will be similar: to derive reading, spelling, or maths estimated scores which show where a child is in relation to other children of the same age and/or grade. They should be psychometrically sound with established normative data, rather than "popular", easy, or currently trendy. Those with good diagnostic components such as provision for analysis of errors in a systematic way, are the most helpful.

Spelling tests available, other than those included in the omnibus tests noted earlier, include the Australian Council for Educational Research (ACER) Grade normed tests for Australian children, and the Schonell Spelling Test (now somewhat out of date but still useful for a rough estimate of "spelling age").

Mathematics. For more detailed assessment of mathematics problems there are fewer well-validated tests available. However Key Math R, as noted in the chapter on MD is very useful for primary school aged children. Key Math, which includes 14 sub-tests, covers three content areas:

- *Basic concepts*, including numeration (e.g. reading and sequencing numbers), rational numbers (fractions, decimals, and

percentages), and geometry (spatial and attribute relationships);
- *operations*, which include addition, subtraction, multiplication, division, and mental computation; and,
- *applications*, which covers measurement, time and money, problem solving involving strategy identification and use, estimation (e.g. suggesting a correct value for an amount misprinted in a newspaper excerpt), and interpreting data such as charts, tables, and graphs.

Scores from this test allow an overall comparison of the child's progress compared with others of the same age/grade, as well as profiles of strength and weakness in each area and across sub-tests and domains. The test is designed to be attractive and motivating for children. It has plenty of variety, with material that varies in difficulty, and allows chances for success even in those with MD. The need for reading is kept to a minimum. It also allows the analysis of written computation which can suggest causes of errors, e.g. why an answer is wrong even if the child appears to understand the concept, such as when figures are mis-aligned or the wrong number is "carried".

Key Math provides helpful information which can be used by teachers to develop more focused procedures for remedial work on specific problem areas. The BAS and the Stanford Binet Test also include mathematical reasoning measures which can provide insights into the child's difficulties in this area.

In summary, these basic assessment tools, directed towards gaining insight into the child's cognitive strengths and weaknesses, together with analysis of the characteristics of his or her particular difficulties with learning one of more of the three Rs, provide the foundation for decisions about what might be required in follow-up assessment which could provide more fine-grained analyses of the problems.

3. Taking the next steps to get more detail on the problems

The best tests incorporate diagnostic information rather than just giving a comparative score. Some tests actually build in diagnostic follow-up tests for children who do very poorly. The Neale Analysis of Reading, for example, has short simple tests of spelling, knowledge of letter names and sounds, auditory discrimination (recognising if two similar words sound the same or different e.g. three and tree), and blending (combining aurally separated sounds to make a word, e.g. b – ring), and discrimination of initial and final sounds of words.

As noted earlier, Key Math also provides considerable diagnostic information, and can be given to children for whom maths is clearly a major and troubling problem.

The assessor can provide a summary and analysis of the nature of the errors and sub-skill deficits and how they contribute to understanding the problems the child is having.

Free writing.   A very diagnostically useful task to give the child is to ask for some free writing. This can be a short story, a paragraph, or even a sentence or two, depending on the age and literacy level of the child. Some children are very reluctant to put pen to paper, and need great encouragement including suggestions for topics. These should be simple and of immediate interest to the child such as weekend activities, "my family", "friends at school" etc.

Information that can be gleaned from the child's spontaneous writing includes: spelling strategies (it is often necessary to get the child to read back what he or she has written to see if the child can understand it and to let you know the origin of badly misspelt words); fine motor skills in pen holding, forming letters, keeping the lines level etc; knowledge of punctuation rules, and the concept of a sentence, which includes use of capital letters and full stops; speed of generation of ideas and words, or the flow of the writing; and ideas and content. Some children will reveal in their writing valuable information about their experiences and feelings which they might not say outright, others have enormous difficulty generating even one sentence. Here is an example from a 9-year-old boy who was referred for aggressive behaviour problems, but who had had no attention from his teachers or parents for his LDs which were identified during behavioural assessment by the psychologist.

Nick's story: **I have frends at school. We have fun to getha sum tim we get in trudel I haf to go to seter Bu Bea and she sox me weth the cain a then I go and play with my frends and play for scre and then the Ball ring a we go in and ta ts the end of my steri.**

Translation: I have friends at school. We have fun together. Some times we get into trouble. I have to go to Sister Barbara and she socks [hits] me with the cane and then I go and play Four Score [a ball game] and then the bell rings and we go in and that's the end of my story.

There are no standard scoring procedures for children's free writing, but this exercise can provide very useful qualitative information about the child's literacy difficulties as the example shows. All of the common problems are illustrated in this example including difficulties with remembering the correct vowels, phonetic approximations, ignorance of vowel digraphs, difficulties with irregular words, limited knowledge of sentence formation, punctuation, use of capital letters etc. Even when older children produce more extended material, showing that they have some writing and compositional abilities, this can be analysed for content level as well as spelling, grammar, and punctuation, and compared with material produced by same age/grade level non SLD children.

Psycholinguistic abilities.   It is very commonly the case that SLD children have basic problems with language in one or more of its many facets. Thus, difficulties in comprehension, expression, articulation, pragmatics (the social, reciprocal, communicative aspects of speech), grammar, and style of language, or some combination of these may underlie learning impairments especially in the reading and spelling area. Further detail on language problems will be provided in Chapter 5, but it is worth including here some notes on one of the most useful tests of selected aspects of psycholinguistic processing, the Illinois Test of Psycholinguistic Abilities (ITPA), (Kirk, McCarthy, & Kirk, 1968). The ITPA is appropriate for children between 2 and 10 years of age; it consists of 12 sub-tests and was constructed to assess both verbal and non-verbal aspects of psycholinguistic ability.

Research with this test has shown that it has a large component of general intelligence; that is, its scores relate strongly to IQ as measured by other tests rather than to specific aspects of language capacities. Accordingly the ITPA cannot be considered a test that *specifically* discriminates amongst facets of language and reading skills as was its authors' intentions. However, it can provide valuable descriptive information about deficiencies in a child's grasp of psycholinguistic functions with some sub-tests being especially useful. For example, the ITPA includes both an auditory memory (digit span) and a visual memory sub-test. The latter, which assesses the ability to remember a series of non-meaningful visual symbols, may give some insight into a child's inability to remember the visual shapes of words from one day to the next, a common complaint of those trying to teach word-recognition skills to RD children. Some comparison between visual and auditory aspects of memory is available within the same standardised assessment.

Another useful sub-test is Verbal Expression which requires the child to develop verbal descriptions of common objects such as a ball and an envelope. Many SLD children have enormous difficulty producing even the most concrete description, illustrating their problems with spontaneous language production and word finding. For such children, it is perhaps no wonder that they have great difficulty in producing written homework which relies on the ability to generate descriptions, facts, and stories.

The ITPA also includes measures of visual discrimination, knowledge of grammatical forms, manual (gestural) expression (e.g. in demonstrating what one does with a hammer), and verbal and visual conceptual ability. The two supplementary tests of auditory closure and sound blending are useful measures of phonological skills. RD children often do very poorly on these two supplementary tests, demonstrating their difficulties with analysing and synthesising the sounds of the language.

When preliminary assessment of intelligence and achievement indicates that the child may be struggling to achieve a level of linguistic competence that is needed to underpin the acquisition of reading and spelling skills, the ITPA can be helpful in giving more detail about the nature of the difficulties. This is particularly the case for children who may produce very little spontaneous conversation, or language samples to allow informal judgement of language development.

Other specific language tests will be noted in the next chapter.

4. An hypothesis-testing model

Once the original referral questions have been addressed, and the estimates of intelligence, cognitive and linguistic strengths and weaknesses have been established as in steps 1, 2, and 3, it is time to consider more specific hypotheses concerning the problems of the individual child. This is the stage for questioning whether there is need for more comprehensive psycholinguistic, neuropsychological, or maths testing to examine in depth the nature and scope of any impairments, and for considering whether a diagnosis of specific LD is appropriate.

Hypotheses of the types illustrated here can be generated and used as the basis of diagnostic decisions, and/or choice of further lines of investigation.

Hypothesis Type 1 — Intellectual disability rather than specific LDs?
In regard to the cognitive profile, the most obvious first question is likely to be: is the child actually functioning at a level below the normal range of intelligence, or has a previously unsuspected level of intellectual disability been identified which might be sufficient to explain why the children is having academic difficulties. If there is reasonable correspondence between the child's overall intellectual ability estimate, and his or her level of progress in learning, one would normally exclude a diagnosis of SLD. Consider the case of an 11-year-old girl who is in Grade 5 but is found to be reading and spelling at a low Grade 2 level. The history suggests that she was slower than average to sit up, to walk,

and to speak in sentences. Her birth weight was well below average. The cognitive assessment shows that her IQ is in the mildly handicapped range, i.e. between 65 and 75. Her reading level is then reasonably consistent with her tested level of ability, and with the suggestions of developmental delay in the history. This child, rather than having an SLD, can be considered to be doing reasonably well given her intellectual capacities. A child who is of below average intelligence who is also reading and writing at a similarly below-average level does not meet the definition for SLD because estimated capacity (IQ) and achievement level are not inconsistent with each other. The learning difficulties are not specific.

In such cases it is sometimes hard for parents, teachers, and other health professionals to realise that intelligence may be below average especially if this is previously unsuspected and the presenting child is verbal, attractive, and socially engaging in a way that can mask real cognitive impairments. Although there may be no specific neuropsychological hypothesising and follow-up testing necessary, some sensitive work is needed to help people in the child's environment to understand and allow for intellectual limitations, to adjust their expectations for academic progress and long-term achievement, and to devise placements and programmes that will maximise potential. This is not to say that further testing to gain more insight into specific cognitive problems may not be useful, but rather that the pathway to enhanced learning outcomes may be somewhat different from that for an SLD child whose intelligence is in the normal or above normal range.

If there is a major discrepancy between what parents and teachers expect and believe that the child is capable of and what his or her intellectual level would predict, this can lead to mismatches between expectations and capabilities, which can make life very difficult for the child, and this mismatch needs to be adjusted. Parents will sometimes reject an assessment of intellectual disability and move on to another professional to look for a more acceptable explanation for the child's difficulties. Although another opinion can be useful, the child who is subjected to repeated testing and investigation is at risk of becoming even more troubled by identification as a "problem" child, and by further experiences of failure, with consequent loss of self-esteem. It is also true that we are dealing with *estimates* of IQ and that the hallmark of childhood is change and development. Hence further progress is always possible, and there is no sense in which this kind of finding is the last word on the child's present or future capacities. It is also important that such a child receives remedial assistance to enhance learning progress.

Other hypotheses that are pertinent at this stage of the formulation when assessment suggests that intelligence is in the normal range, centre around influences such as apparent poor motivation for school work, perhaps boredom, incompatibility with a particular teacher, or resistance to parents' pressure to work harder. These psychosocial aspects all need to be explored in a clinical interview and via behavioural assessment and analysis if this seems warranted, before proceeding to more cognitive assessments.

Hypothesis Type 2 — Specific neuropsychological problems.   For a child whose performance clearly falls within the average or above range, the next step is to consider the profile of strengths and weaknesses obtained from tests like the WISC, along with the details of the problem history, and to develop hypotheses about underlying processing problems which may be explored via neuropsychological tests.

For example, there may be evidence of problems in visual or auditory perception, and/or memory; difficulties with focusing and sustaining attention, limited scanning or checking of material to be processed; planning and organisational strategy limitations; problems with language comprehension and expression; extreme slowness in information processing; evidence of weak or absent phonological skills; motor deficits; problem-solving limitations; or difficulties in learning and generalising strategies for reading or mathematics tasks. Further assessment to analyse in more detail any such hypothesised difficulties is desirable at this stage.

An example of such a case might be the following. A 9-year-old boy presenting with school learning problems is shown to have a Performance IQ of 128, a verbal IQ of 94 (which includes a very low Vocabulary score) and he is three years behind his age-expected level in reading. He is, in fact, only at the beginning stages of reading, and can scarcely write and spell at all. His developmental history suggests that he was slow to talk, had difficulties in making himself understood, and has always been interested in doing and making things, rejecting all encouragement to read with his parents, to listen to stories, or to talk about his daily doings. The hypothesis here might be that this is an RD child with excellent fluid intelligence, whose problems relate to developmental difficulties with language. These have led him to avoid language-related activities and to concentrate on his strengths with more manipulative construction tasks. In order to understand more about the precise nature of his language and reading difficulties, follow-up testing would focus on diagnostic language tests involving comprehension, expression, articulation, phonological knowledge, and verbal memory, as well as in-depth assessment of his understanding of letters and word analysis strategies.

Hypothesis Type 3 — Psychological and behavioural factors   The qualitative data gained from observing and interacting with the child is invaluable to add to the results of testing and to help in generating hypotheses. Such data include evidence of anxiety, lack of confidence, hasty decision making, reluctance to try or to guess when answers are uncertain, shyness and poverty of language in conversation, preoccupation with personal or family concerns, fidgetiness and inability to sit still, fear of failure, over confidence, etc.

These are not necessarily alternatives to Type 1 or Type 2 hypotheses but they may be significant factors in the child's failure to learn satisfactorily and they need thorough exploration.

Consider the case of a 10-year-old boy with an overall IQ of 100 but with reading and arithmetic skills two and a half years behind his current grade level. His memory for digits is very weak and his score on a symbolic coding test is well below average, mostly because he did not trouble to draw the symbols accurately, and was very impulsive and disorganised in his approach. His parents and teachers report that he can be very quick, bright, and knowledgeable sometimes and appears to have good academic potential, but he never sits still, does not pay attention to instructions or requests, and seems unable to concentrate for more than a few moments. During testing he was hard to manage and to keep on task; he fidgeted with his clothes and the test equipment, got bored with each sub-test very quickly, and refused to keep trying after a couple of failures. He was constantly asking if the session was finished so that he could go outside.

The hypothesis here would be that his hyperactive, disorganised, and distractible behaviour was interfering with his ability to cope with classroom instruction, and that his true potential was hard to estimate. Home and school observations would be helpful in gaining a more systematic picture of his behaviour, and special conditions and techniques might be needed in further testing of his abilities. These might include increasing his motivation by the use of rewards for concentration and cooperation, and using brief, highly structured testing sessions, along with absolute firmness and consistency in supervising set tasks. For this case, both behavioural and learning potential require comprehensive assessment and this should be followed up by suggestions for strategies to deal with both sets of difficulties.

COMMUNICATING THE FINDINGS

A major challenge of any assessment of SLDs is in the final outcome of the process, which is:

a)   to communicate clearly the nature of the difficulties for the individual child to parents, teachers, and any other involved professionals, and:

b)   to use the formulations developed through the assessment to provide well-informed specific suggestions for remediation of the problems, and ways of optimising the potential of the child.

Parents and child need to understand why the child is failing to learn at the expected rate, what are the particular difficulties he or she is having with various aspects of learning, what might underlie those difficulties, and how to help in the future.

Finding ways to help the child to feel confident, competent, and valued is perhaps the most important long-term goal to focus on. Gathering resources, whether from within the family, the school, or from outside experts, to work towards improving learning progress is the next most important goal.

All children have competencies in some area of their lives; the SLDs should not be permitted to dominate their self-image. Whether it is sport, music, mechanical ability, helpfulness, care of animals, model building, drawing, gardening, or any other skill is immaterial. It is essential to find a focus or an area of activity where the child feels he or she is competent, and valuable, and for people to tell the child this, and to encourage him or her to further develop such interests and skills. This does not mean that the LDs are neglected, just that there is more to life than school work and one's significance and self-worth can develop in many different ways. Sometimes parents look puzzled or blank when they are asked what their SLD child is good at, or where he or she has shown enthusiastic interest, because they have become so focused on the deficiencies of the child's school progress. However with a little thought they can always come up with some positives, and these must be highlighted for further encouragement and development. In this way the psychological well-being of the child does not get lost in an over-riding emphasis on problem analyses and remedial prescriptions.

Teachers will want to understand why the child has been proceeding through school without keeping up, or why he or she seems unable to complete homework and read set books, or is continually acting the clown in class, (or alternatively is sad and withdrawn, with low self-esteem). A comprehensive assessment covering behaviour and learning problems which can provide the basis for a revised learning programme that takes into account strengths and weaknesses in the child's profile is what the teacher is usually seeking. For example, if phonological skills in reading are weak, and visual capacities are strong, the learning programme can emphasise and build on the strengths while at the same time attempting to put in place strategies to develop weak areas, especially when they are critical to further progress in reading. Teachers can often benefit from enhanced understanding of the relationship between the behavioural and cognitive aspects of a child's problems as a result of a good psychological assessment, so that they can adapt their teaching programme to provide a better-structured environment to cope with diverse socio-emotional as well as learning needs.

Written reports for the family and the school which set out clearly and simply the formulation of the problems, along with recommendations for action need to be provided. Such reports should be free of jargon and technical professional language which is hard to understand. Written reports are often best presented first through face-to-face meetings with all involved, to explain the results of the assessment and the meaning of any diagnosis. This provides an opportunity for everyone to ask questions, express their doubts or concerns, to receive counselling and encouragement, and for mutual feedback. It is also a time to explore strategies for identifying or generating remedial resources for the child. Follow-up with family and school and continuing collaboration between teachers, family, and clinician over the long term to see that appropriate help has been found, and that the child is making gains in problem areas, will be an important support for future progress.

SUMMARY

Assessment should be sensitive to the needs and expectations of the child, the family, and the school. Basic history taking should be followed by a standardised cognitive assessment which will provide a profile of strengths and weaknesses. Tests of literacy and/or numeracy which are directed towards the particular referral problems should follow. An hypothesis-testing approach helps to focus thinking about the most reasonable diagnosis, and about what kinds of additional assessment would provide more detailed analysis of suspected cognitive, language, or other difficulties. Communicating the results of assessment in clear and practical terms, and in ways that facilitate discussion of options for remedial assistance is critically important.

CHAPTER FIVE

Neuropsychology and its uses in understanding learning difficulties

Neuropsychology has become particularly important and useful in the understanding of LDs over the last 15 or 20 years. In fact, the need to try to understand the nature and origins of LDs has provided a major impetus for the growth of interest in child neuropsychology, so each set of interests has enriched the other.

Put most simply, neuropsychology is about the study of the relationships between the anatomical, neurological, and other biological characteristics of the brain, and individual behaviour, or performance. It includes the study of the specialised functions of specific parts of the brain in influencing behaviour or performance; and it examines the ways in which neurological, biological, and functional aspects of the brain are translated into actual human thoughts and actions. It also includes detailed analysis of the cognitive processing strategies that people use in problem solving, such as the ways in which a person tries to reproduce a complex visual stimulus involving planning and organisational skills and attention to detail.

The methods used in this rapidly developing discipline, which overlaps and integrates with knowledge from psychology, psychiatry, and neurology, depend heavily on the administration of tests or specific tasks to individuals, to measure the quantitative and qualitative aspects of their behaviour under particular task conditions. Neuropsychologists then try to make inferences about the relationship between observed test behaviour of the individual, and the parts of the brain that are believed to be involved in the learning or performance which is measured by such tasks, and to make inferences about possible sites of brain damage or dysfunction which could be responsible for observed deficits in behaviour.

Often this is done by matching up the results of task performance with scans of the brain which may show particular sites of damage. The particular damage is then presumed to be associated with the behavioural or performance deficits that appear on cognitive and problem-solving tasks. This is the basic theory underpinning neuropsychology, although in practice this is a challenging way of trying to find windows into the brain, and some might say that there is still as much "art" as science in the interpretation of neuropsychological relationships.

BACKGROUND TO THE DEVELOPMENT OF NEUROPSYCHOLOGY

The accumulation of knowledge in this area has been based on both animal and human studies of:

a) The specific behaviours of individuals after they have sustained some kind of brain damage, where the locality of the damage can be established, usually by scanning techniques, or where there has been brain investigation and/or surgery to remove a tumour, repair damage, or alleviate epileptic seizures.

   In animal experimental studies it has been possible to remove a certain part of the brain and then measure the effects on subsequent behaviour. For example, damaging or destroying parts of the amygdala and the hippocampus, in the central area of the brain, leads to severe memory difficulties in both humans and monkeys, although there may be preserved ability to learn new skills and habits. Some of the monkey work shows very specific effects of lesions in one area of the brain which produce deficits on some learning tasks but not others, even though the tasks may, on the surface, appear quite similar.

b) Studies of the performance of "normal" and brain-damaged human subjects presented with learning tasks where the input to specific parts of the brain is controlled in some way, e.g. in so-called "dichotic listening" or "visual half-field" studies.

In *dichotic listening studies*, two different auditory stimuli are presented via headphones, to each ear at the same time (e.g. dog to the left and log to the right). The major auditory pathways going from each ear to each half of the brain are crossed, hence the side of the brain that is more prepared for, or dominant in, processing a particular stimulus should receive the input from the opposite ear more quickly and be more accurate in recognising it.

For example, if the word "dog" is heard in the right ear, and the message then crosses to the left hemisphere (which is specialised for processing language), it should be more quickly recognised than the word "log" going to the left ear and crossing to the right (non-language) hemisphere.

The strongest examples of this effect are found in the language area where it is known that for most individuals, language is predominantly located in the left hemisphere of the brain. If a person is consistently faster and more accurate with information presented to one ear, it is concluded that the contralateral or opposite hemisphere has a special ability to process that type of stimulus. When there is damage to one side of the brain or the other, these normally lateralised relationships can be disrupted. Studies of clinical cases where such damage has been sustained, and disruption to normal processing has occurred, provide another kind of evidence that can be matched up with the experimental findings with normal populations.

Visual half-field studies are based on a parallel set of neuropsychological assumptions. All visual pathways in the brain are crossed, hence stimuli presented to one visual half-field are received first by the contralateral or opposite side of the brain—left going across to right, and right going across to left.

Techniques have been developed which can organise and control the input of material to be visually processed, to one side of the brain or another, thus allowing some control over which hemisphere first receives stimuli. As with the dichotic listening technique, such studies have been useful in showing which side of the brain preferentially processes which kinds of stimuli. These are called laterality studies.

In summary, this genre of neuropsychological work suggests that the left hemisphere specialises in dealing with language, symbolic, and temporally/sequentially ordered stimuli; while the right hemisphere is specialised for environmental sounds, visuo-spatial material, and "Gestalt" or holistic perception and processing. When SLD children show difficulties with particular types of material, or apparent abnormal laterality patterns on these specially designed tasks, it is often hypothesised that one side or other of the brain is not functioning normally. Such hypotheses have most commonly been applied to explanations of reading difficulties, where it is suggested that the left side of the brain has not adequately developed its expected language and reading functions.

Despite the plausible nature of these hypotheses, there is little consistent clinical or experimental evidence that SLD children are slower to develop brain lateralisation, or specialised left hemisphere language functioning, or that they have identifiable defects on one side of the brain or the other. So this type of hypothesis remains unconfirmed. Similar doubts are relevant in suggested connections between handedness and SLDs. Many years ago it was believed that RD was related to being left-handed, but this theory no longer has credence. A variety of problems with learning and development may be related to uncertain handedness, or delay in developing secure hand preference, but there is no evidence to suggest that left- or mixed-handedness has any causal connection to SLDs.

There are also theories relating particular processing or learning dysfunctions to other parts of the brain, the parietal or the frontal lobes for example. Children with attention-regulation problems, poor planning and organisation skills, and who are limited, rigid, and inflexible in their approaches to problems, are hypothesised to have problems with frontal lobe functioning. However, again, this work is speculative and there is no strong evidence to implicate the frontal lobes specifically in the problems of SLD children. Such theories must be especially tentative, as in most cases SLD children have no known neurological damage.

The various aspects of neuropsychology, including laterality or hemisphere functioning, comprise a complex, currently much researched area which needs at least a whole book of its own in relation to the understanding of SLD. In providing a summary of neuropsychological aspects, this limited outline is intended simply to sensitise the reader to an area of developing knowledge which contributes to theories of brain-behaviour relationships with some relevance to SLDs.

THEORIES AND METHODS EXPLORING
BRAIN DYSFUNCTION IN SLD

There have been many recent attempts to understand what specific behavioural and brain processes might underlie the difficulties some children experience in learning, by using methods and techniques developed in human neuropsychology. There is an assumption inherent in the definition of SLDs that some brain processes have gone awry, or are deficient in some way, and that such dysfunction has a causal role in the SLDs. However, most SLD children show no outward sign of any kind of quantifiable neurological damage, and even a thorough paediatric examination often fails to reveal any abnormalities. Moreover, even when there are some abnormalities found (such as extreme clumsiness or poor motor co-ordination, or language deficits), it is often unclear where these come from, how they are connected neurologically, and how they are related in a direct causal sense to the individual child's SLDs.

This is a very difficult field of study because even the most modern scanning techniques may fail to reveal brain damage that is actually there. Conversely, when neurological examination or scanning does show some abnormalities, there are not necessarily any observable behavioural or learning consequences. Children with a wide variety of problems, including some psychiatric or behavioural disorders, may show "minor" signs of brain damage whether they have SLDs or not. Hence, the significance of neurological signs in children, unless they are gross (as for example in identified epilepsy), remains somewhat of a mystery.

Minimal brain damage

Much has been written about "Minimal Brain Damage" or MBD. This is a term used by those who believe firmly in a neurological or biological basis for learning disorders (and in some cases for behavioural disorders such as Attention Deficit Disorder with Hyperactivity, as well). MBD is believed to be reflected by so-called "soft signs" of neurological abnormality, including such indications as mild tremor, oddities in posture or gait, clumsiness, word-finding difficulties, abnormal reflexes, left /right confusions, overflow or mirror movements, to name only a few. Such signs are common in very young children, indeed they are normative in early development; but as the child matures and gains motor and cognitive control, they will disappear, usually by the age of 8 at the latest. It is worth noting that many adults will report that they have such problems as left/right confusion even though there is no sign that they have a neurological or psychological disorder, so the significance of these signs even in adulthood is obscure.

Because in so many SLD cases it is impossible to find evidence for neurological or biological problems or abnormalities, MBD proponents make the claim that they must be there, but are too subtle or "minimal" for us to be able to identify them on the basis of current investigative methods. The term MBD, then, is used to describe what is actually only an hypothesis, and one that has minimal explanatory value for SLD because we are uncertain what these signs mean other than as indices of some immaturity in development if they persist past the early childhood phase. This kind of MBD theorising has been described as neuro-mythologising. At the least, it is unhelpful in understanding

SLDs, and at worst it misleads people into believing that the problems are "medical" or biological and should therefore have medical intervention. As there are no successful medical or pharmacological treatments for SLDs, such beliefs can be maladaptive.

Electrophysiological and brain imaging methods

There have been many attempts at electrophysiological and neuro-imaging investigations of SLD children in the search for biological abnormalities. Neuro-imaging methods used include Computerised Axial Tomography (CAT) scans which provide images of the brain and skull to allow the search for signs of lesions or abnormalities; and Positron Emission Tomography (PET) and Regional Cerebral Blood Flow studies. In this latter method the person has a radioactive compound injected into the bloodstream which will concentrate in areas of the brain that are particularly active while the person is asked to carry out specified cognitive operations such as calculating or word-finding. The concentration of activity can be picked up through imaging techniques that show which parts of the brain are involved in processing differing kinds of material. Such techniques are considered promising but are still relatively imprecise, and have not as yet offered much enlightenment about the nature or source of any possible relevant brain mechanisms underlying SLD.

Magnetic Resonance Imaging (MRI), which is a newer technique similar to PET scans but without involving injection of radioactive substances, provides more finely resolved images to assist in finding abnormalities. But even with this technique, little has been discovered about any structural anomalies specific to SLD children.

Electroencephalography (EEG) is a technique for recording and amplifying the electrical discharges within the brain, using electrodes placed on the scalp. There have been many of these kinds of investigations in SLD children, with mixed results. Any particular electrophysiological abnormalities found are usually not specific to SLD as distinct from other kinds of disorders that are thought to involve brain function, and the methods are unable to distinguish between particular types of SLDs.

Evoked potentials (EPs) of both visual and auditory types can also be used to explore brain function. After placement of electrodes on the scalp, subjects are presented with auditory or visual stimuli and, as they watch or listen, the electrical responses of the brain can be recorded through these scalp electrodes. Similar findings to those suggested earlier for EEG investigations, i.e. non-specific abnormalities, can sometimes be observed, but they add disappointingly little to our understanding of SLDs.

Overall, the findings relevant to understanding SLDs, using the techniques outlined here have been described as "provocative, but scattered, and inconsistent results" (Morris, Levy, & Pirozzolo, 1988, p.363). Any possible biological causes remain a mystery for most SLD cases.

USES OF NEUROPSYCHOLOGICAL ASSESSMENT IN SLD CHILDREN

The most useful outcome of paediatric neurological or neuropsychological assessment is not in speculating about the possible existence or origins of any brain dysfunction, but in gaining a clearer picture of current functioning using diagnostic tests, which can help in formulating rational management programmes. The rationale for deciding to carry out a neuropsychological assessment of an SLD child includes:

- differential diagnosis, i.e. identification of the specific individual problems that allow a diagnosis of a particular type of disorder;
- obtaining a clear profile of strengths and weaknesses in cognitive capacities;
- guiding intervention and management plans;
- allowing observation and monitoring of change and development over time as a consequence of intervention; and,
- for research purposes, to contribute to the further understanding of SLDs and neuropsychological associations in general.

A neuropsychological assessment is not likely to comprehensively explain the underlying problems for SLD children, not only because of the powerful influence of environmental and experiential factors in the history of the child and in his or her day-to-day behaviour, but also because we do not have the means to confidently establish correspondence between deficits as shown on tests and dysfunction in particular parts of the brain. Nevertheless such assessment can be extremely helpful in understanding the *nature of the processing difficulties* that an individual may be experiencing, even if this does not provide a clear window into the brain.

A good assessment can show which particular abilities are compromised, and which ones are intact or age-appropriate. The astute clinician can then go on to suggest how the deficits identified may be related to academic problems, how they might be remedied, or how the strengths shown in the profile can be emphasised in ways that will facilitate more successful learning.

NEUROPSYCHOLOGICAL THEORIES OF READING
AND MATHEMATICAL DISABILITIES

More than a century ago, researchers were speculating about the relationship between SLDs and neurological abnormalities (Jackson, 1874/1932, cited in Tramontana & Hooper, 1988). Orton, in 1937, suggested that language and reading difficulties were due to problems with establishing the normal dominance of the left or language hemisphere. Although this hypothesis has been developed and researched during this century, Orton's claims have not been supported by scientific evidence.

Developing and testing theories concerning which particular processing difficulties might underlie SLDs has been an extremely difficult undertaking, in part because of the seemingly intractable problems of satisfactorily agreeing on what we mean by SLDs. Greater progress in understanding has been made in areas where researchers have developed and tested detailed theories about specific kinds of cognitive processing such as accuracy of word recognition, or how children achieve the spelling of words, or decode unfamiliar words. To look at SLDs without pinpointing the specific learning deficits would be like looking for needles in haystacks.

Basically the available theories about reading, spelling, and writing problems fall into three classes. There are those in which the focus is on *visuospatial problems* which may hinder children from perceiving, analysing, and remembering visual material such as words and numbers. As reading and writing appear at least on the surface to be visually mediated skills it is easy to see why the eyes are often the first feature that is suspected of going wrong.

The second class of theories is focused on *auditory memory problems* (e.g. Jorm, 1983), which some have claimed underlie reading difficulties; that is, the RD child cannot accurately perceive and remember what he or she hears, and thus memory for letters and words, for the order of words, or any other information involving the auditory memory system for that matter, is impaired. Consequently, sequentially ordered material such as language or print is very difficult to process and comprehend. It is widely claimed that memory problems in RD children are specific to tasks that require the use of phonological processes (e.g. Share, 1995).

More recent theories of SLD have emphasised "working memory" as playing an important role in learning disorders. Working memory refers to the particular brain systems that are involved in the short-term storage of information while cognitive tasks are being carried out (as in reading and calculating for example). This is different from long-term memory which refers to stored memories that can be called up after a period of time has elapsed. Children may show working memory problems for many different reasons, including attention deficits that interfere with receiving and rehearsing the information needed to solve a problem. Language problems may also handicap the receiving, coding, and storing of speech or print information needed for reading. The pathway could also go in reverse, with working memory problems leading to language problems. Or, both sets of difficulties could be the consequence of another factor such as auditory perception problems. Hence, although it is true that SLD children often show working memory problems, it is uncertain how these arise or how they impinge on the learning problems they have. Recent research by Swanson (1993, 1994) has been aimed at differentiating the influence of short-term memory (STM), and working memory (WM) for children and adults with SLDs on differing aspects of academic skills. Although STM and WM contributed, via separate factors, to reading comprehension and to mathematics performance, STM had little influence on word recognition. Swanson (1993) also reported that SLD children had poorer WM than non-LD children of similar age. RD and MD children did not differ on verbal and visual-spatial WM measures. This kind of experimental work underlines the challenges of trying to find SLD-specific memory problems and the need to be cautious and discriminating in making claims about memory-based explanations of SLDs.

For children with RDs there is clear evidence that they have particular problems with memory for phonologically encoded material, but whether this is cause or effect of the RDs is uncertain. Recent evidence suggests that it may be both (Byrne & Fielding-Barnsley, 1993). Nor is there any neurological evidence relating to memory impairments in RD children which could provide explanations for their difficulties. Thus although it is not difficult to demonstrate working memory deficits in RD children experimentally, neuropsychological theories relating RDs to memory problems are still poorly specified at this stage.

The third type of theory asserts that RDs are the consequence of general or specific *language problems*, such as impoverished vocabulary, or knowledge of the meaning aspects of language; or difficulties in analysing the sounds of the language and putting them together to understand and remember words and sentences. One example of such a theory is the argument that children with speech problems, such as poor ability to articulate or pronounce words correctly, have inaccurate sound representations of words in their heads and that this handicaps them in matching up a word that they see, with a word that is in their mental dictionary. So for example, if their mental auditory representation of the word "that" is "vat", they will be lost when they read the combination of letters "T H A T" and try to match it up with a word that they know.

Language deficits are strong candidates as antecedents to RDs; it is well documented that many RD children have a history of language problems before they began to read (Vellutino, 1979). However this association is not inevitable, as there are also RD individuals who have an apparently normal history of language development, who are articulate, have good verbal memories, and good vocabularies, but still have severe difficulties with print.

In regard to maths disorders there is little coherent neuro-psychological theory, but a number of researchers have suggested that the neuropsychological pattern for specific maths computation disorder involves weaknesses in perceptual organisational abilities, (e.g. poor performance on the Tactual Performance Test, the Beery Visual Motor Integration Test, and WISC sub-tests loading on spatial ability such as Block Design and Object Assembly). On paper, SMD children cannot keep columns in line, do not read signs correctly, and get confused about direction (Strang & Rourke, 1985). Rourke and Del Dotto (1994) claim that they have identified patterns of "material-specific" strengths and weaknesses in children with diverse reading and mathematical problems and that there may be neurophysiological differences shown in evoked potential studies. But they do concede that this claim requires more evidence and especially more attention to the relationships between ability profiles and intervention methods.

General language impairments can also underlie problems with mathematical reasoning, and this in turn limits exposure to and experience with arithmetic processes. Language capacity should be a focus in a thorough neuropsychological assessment of any presenting SLD.

As is the case with RD, working memory deficits have been suggested as a cause of SMD. Although it has been proposed that some children have circumscribed problems with working memory for numbers, it seems unlikely that broader language influences can be excluded from arithmetical tasks involving memory. Furthermore, problems with the storage of numerical information in long-term memory is likely to play a role in any observed deficits in problem solving. Siegel and Ryan (1988), have claimed that children with specific arithmetic disabilities show working memory deficits only on counting tasks, i.e. problems with processing complex and novel visual stimuli. Problems with learning and retrieval of basic arithmetic facts from long-term memory, even after much drill and practice, have also been highlighted (Geary, 1993).

Although memory factors are undoubtedly important in their association with SLDs, it is uncertain whether they are causal in their relationships. Training children in short-term memory skills does not appear to have beneficial effects on cognitive abilities such as reading and arithmetic. Nevertheless, identification of memory limitations is important in neuropsychological assessment, because it can be helpful in devising more successful teaching and learning strategies. For example, avoiding long complex instructions, presenting material in short chunks, and getting children to focus on and then to repeat back instructions can help children with memory limitations.

The theories noted here will be explicated in more detail in the next sections.

Visuospatial and perceptual theories

There has been ongoing debate for many years about just what perceptual processes or functions might be deficient or malfunctioning in RD children. Because reading, on the surface, appears to be a visual skill it seems obvious to look for visual impairments that might impede progress. The fact that children reverse letters like b and d, or sequences of letters (saw for was) suggests immediately that there is a problem with visual sequencing. But the fact is that reversals are common in young children learning to read, i.e. those whose knowledge of letters and sequences is still insecure. They are not a sign of disability but of an immature stage in the learning process.

Hence theories of RD in particular, which emphasise the diagnostic and neuropsychological significance of letter and word reversals can be misleading. Young children learning to read commonly make these errors—not all RD children make them, some do sometimes but not always, so these characteristics are not especially related to RD, but most probably to the particular developmental stage of learning to read. By this argument it would be predicted that the more closely the reading of an RD child approximated that of a younger unskilled reader, the more likely it would be that reversal errors would be found.

Theories of reading disability based on visual impairments have always had their adherents and probably always will. They are particularly active currently amongst optometrists who present themselves as "behavioural optometrists" and take it upon themselves to give psychological tests, make diagnoses, and provide (untested and apparently ineffective) remedial "eye skilling" programmes. Scientific research has shown that children who have poor visuo-spatial or visuo-perceptual skills are *not* at higher risk for RD than are children without these problems (see e.g. Vellutino, 1978). The majority of RD children are characterised by language rather than perceptual/visual problems.

Another popular theory, that of "cross modal" deficiencies, or "intersensory integration" i.e. problems integrating information across modalities such as sight, hearing and touch—has also not stood up to empirical testing. Vellutino's (1978) review of experimental work in this field concluded that although it is possible to find differences between RD and normal children on cross modal tasks, it is not clear what this means for problems in reading. Many of the tests used in this work were confounded by short-term memory requirements, and verbal coding ability. Where studies have controlled for these factors through using non-verbal tasks, few differences between RD and non-RD children in cross modal processing have been shown. The relative dearth of recent published research in this particular domain suggests that the theory is out of favour, as a result of its failure to explain much about why and how children fail to read adequately.

LANGUAGE PROBLEMS IN RD CHILDREN

The most substantial and consistent body of evidence implicates language deficiencies as the most significant underlying factors in SLD.

First, children who have developmental speech and language problems are particularly at risk for reading and spelling problems. Second, most SLD children show a variety of problems with language-based tests and tasks, but few of them have equivalent difficulties with non-linguistic tasks. That is, their disabilities seem clearly related to language processes. Children who begin school with very impoverished vocabularies and limited command of language are handicapped as they begin their instruction in reading. Their restricted mental dictionaries mean that they do not securely know many words that they are then asked to read. Many of them have problems with word-finding and naming tasks especially under time pressure, suggesting that they have problems retrieving phonological representations of words, even when they know them. Serial naming tasks are even more problematic for them (Share, 1995).

Failure to master reading skills often sets such children further behind, as they have reduced access to an avenue of language learning that is available to children who are reading normally. Their difficulties are compounded.

Siegel (1985) has reported evidence that RD children show numerous expressive language deficits, e.g. in the ability to perceive spoken sounds, to blend sounds to make words, to name objects, letters, numbers, and colours, especially at speed; in the ability to process and use the semantic and syntactic aspects of language; difficulties with the complex and irregular aspects of language, as well as phonological problems. Other language-processing problems commonly reported in RD children include speech perception impairments, and sentence memory and comprehension deficits, supporting theories of language weaknesses as critical in the risk for RD.

RD children often have much lower scores on tests of verbal intelligence such as vocabulary or word definition, by comparison with their performance on tests involving analysis and synthesis of visuo-spatial material such as block designs or jigsaw tasks. However, this is not always true, as many SLD children show difficulties spread across both areas and may have a very uneven profile of abilities as assessed in standard intelligence tests.

RD children may also show poor performance on tasks such as learning and remembering lists of linguistic stimuli such as words, letters, numbers, syllables, and sentences. This is the case whether the linguistic material is presented through the visual or the auditory modality. It is *verbal memory* that is the problem.

It has been persuasively argued that this problem arises for RD children because they have difficulty perceiving, retaining, and using phonetic or sound-based representations of language (Mann & Brady, 1988). Because it is possible to observe these effects in young (RD) children *before* they learn to read, it is claimed that such deficiencies may play a causal role (see Chapter 2). Bryant and Bradley's (1985) work showing that early phonological skills in normal children predicted reading ability three or more years later, and Byrne and Fielding-Barnsley's (1995) demonstration of the benefits of teaching phonological skills at pre-school age on reading two years later, further support the arguments about the centrality of these capacities in learning to read.

SUB-TYPES OF SLDs

Another way of trying to understand underlying deficits in SLD children and how they might interact to contribute to the SLDs, is to examine large groups of children to see if they can be sub-grouped in some way that will help to understand their difficulties. The long-term aim of this kind of work would be to match up treatment methods to groups of children showing clusters of similar deficits.

Children with SLDs are very heterogeneous, in terms of the specific problems they have with learning. Although we can develop and evaluate theories about the underlying nature of difficulties in the process of learning to read, once we come to consider the individual, it is clear that there is huge variation, with every child having his or her own distinct profile of strengths and weaknesses. This makes it inordinately difficult to claim that any one explanation is relevant or that any one treatment will meet the needs of all SLD children. We can find sub-groups of children who primarily have problems with just spelling, or with just maths, or (very occasionally) just reading, but in fact these children are rare. In addition, within the particular SLD category, e.g. SMD, children vary in their level of skills with different aspects of that learning area. Hence it is a difficult undertaking to try to put children in categories or neat "boxes" which would be helpful in finding specific treatments appropriate for each category.

Nevertheless, much of the neuropsychological research with SLD children has been focused on finding particular profiles of assets and deficits which might be able to explain the problems not only of individuals but of groups of individuals with similar problems. Since the 1960s, there have been numerous studies specifically concerned with trying to identify sub-types, i.e. clusters of children who can be identified on the basis of particular shared cognitive characteristics. More than 100 of these sub-classification type studies have been published over the past 30 years (see Hooper & Willis, 1989, for a summary).

Working with large samples of SLD children, researchers administer batteries of tests including measures of neuropsychological functioning such as Word Fluency or Auditory Memory along with measures of maths, reading, and spelling skills (see the work of Lyon, Moats, & Flynn, 1988, for a typical example of this kind of research, and also Hooper & Willis, 1989). Reading-related tests might include word naming, sound blending and word segmentation, memory for letters, numbers, words and sentences, sentence repetition and completion, and reading of nonsense words (e.g. "mun").

Measures of visual-spatial and sequencing ability are usually also included, such as analysis, synthesis, and memory for visual patterns and sequences of non-verbal symbols. Standard neuropsychological tests of the kinds outlined in a later section are also included as part of a very comprehensive battery of tests in these studies.

Typical sub-types or clusters of SLD children which have emerged from these studies have included:

Group 1: children characterised by problems with language comprehension, phoneme blending, visual-spatial and visual memory skills, visual-motor integration, along with strengths in naming and auditory discrimination skills. Children in this group were deficient in both whole word recognition and word attack abilities.

Group 2:   children with a similar pattern of mixed deficits but they were milder than in group 1.

Group 3:   children showing specific deficits in language comprehension and sound blending, but strengths in other linguistic and visual perceptual skills; their reading errors were mostly of the phonetic type.

Group 4:   children with problems with visual-motor integration tasks but average performance on all other measures. Reading errors were mixed but there were particular problems with irregular words (words that cannot be directly sounded out to make sense, such as "friend").

Group 5:   these children had deficits in language comprehension, auditory memory, and sound blending, with strengths in all visual perceptual areas. They had very poor phonetic skills in reading and spelling.

Group 6:   these children showed no particular cognitive deficits at all despite their SLDs, hence assessment did not illuminate their underlying problems.

The identification of these particular sub-types (Lyon et al., 1988) demonstrates that: severity of problems is very variable (compare Groups 1 and 2 and Group 6); that there is a group of children whose problems seem confined to visual processing (see Group 4 which comprised about 30% of children in this study), and this seems related to memory for irregular words; and that language and phonological problems are common in the majority of children with SLDs, across most sub-types.

Other researchers have reported broadly similar results in their sub-typing attempts (see Taylor, Fletcher, & Satz, 1982).

Vellutino, Scanlon, and Tanzman (1991) have looked at ways of building bridges between neuropsychological and cognitive conceptualisations of RD. They also looked for sub-types amongst RD children on the basis of their abilities in phonological, semantic, and visual capacities. They identified a large-sub group whose main problems were in phonological decoding, another containing children with problems in all three areas, and another where the children were adequate in all three areas despite their RD. Few of their RD children had problems only with visual analysis, or only with vocabulary. This work suggested that not all domains of language are equally influential in the development of RD, and it is consistent with the emphasis on phonological skills as playing a causal role in RDs.

Some researchers have also tried to assess the relevance of sub-types for particular remedial approaches (e.g. Lyon et al., 1988). This is clearly a strategic way of going about relating skill deficits and strengths to prescription of intervention. Success with this approach has been limited, in part because of the influence of severity of SLDs which may override particular connections between neuropsychological profiles and teaching methods; it is probably also in part because of lack of expertise in devising teaching programmes that are effective (see Chapter 7).

CONNECTIONS TO "ACQUIRED" SYNDROMES OF COGNITIVE DEFICITS

Another recently developed way of analysing and categorising the cognitive neuropsychological characteristics of children with reading and spelling difficulties has been to ask whether their problems are similar to those shown by patients with various syndromes of "acquired dyslexia". For example, there have been a number of single-case studies that provide detailed analyses of the error types found in RD children and compare them with errors on the same tests found in brain-damaged adults (e.g. Coltheart et al., 1983; Prior & McCorriston, 1985). These kinds of studies have been used to test specific theories about the ways in which words are stored and accessed in the brain, with the aim of constructing a cognitive neuropsychological model of word knowledge. The "dual route theory" as noted in Chapter 2, for example, explains how patterns of errors in reading regular, irregular, and nonsense words can suggest the existence of different routes from print to meaning in the linguistic processing systems in the brain.

Castles and Coltheart (1993) have recently tested their cognitive neuropsychological theories of "varieties of dyslexia" with a large group of RD children. Most of their cases had difficulties with *both* the *direct* route to word recognition (visual recognition pathway going directly to accessing meaning), and the *indirect* route (use of phonological translation skills to construct the word before accessing the meaning system). But they did find small RD sub-groups who were similar to children *without* reading problems, i.e. at a normal skill level in their facility with one or the other route (sometimes called reading by eye or by ear), whilst being deficient in the other. These sub-groups with specific deficits were considered to be developmental examples of "surface" and "phonological dyslexia", similar in characteristics to adults with these acquired reading disorders in the way that they translated print to meaning.

This genre of research is providing more detailed analyses of the kinds of stimulus-specific errors made by both adult and child cases of reading disability, and provides a basis for assessment and analysis of the particular reading difficulties of the individual child. Hopefully it will lead to the availability of better-targeted remedial approaches which ought to match deficits to treatment. It has been central to recent advances in understanding of word recognition and production in reading and spelling.

In summary, many researchers have shown that it is possible to identify sub-groups of SLD children who share similar problems in reading and/or spelling, and/or mathematics, and that it is possible to differentiate between clusters of cases, on the basis of particular types of language or other neuropsychological impairments which may be related to their difficulties. It is fair to say, however, that groups generally vary in *severity* of SLDs as much as in kind; that it is not easy to reliably replicate the sub-groups from one population to the next (although the best of the sub-typing research does attempt this); and that we still have to demonstrate the relationships between sub-group membership and either longer-term outcome, or response to treatment.

THE NEUROPSYCHOLOGY
OF MATHEMATICS DISORDERS

Despite the comments made in Chapter 3 concerning the hypothesised associations between brain lesion sites and SMD *in adults*, it is generally agreed that there is little evidence concerning such relationships in children with this kind of SLD. There are a few case histories documenting the loss of certain abilities after brain trauma in childhood (see Ashcraft, Yamashita, & Aram, 1992), but for the majority of SMD children whose difficulties are developmental rather than acquired, and which have no known biological origins, there is little more than speculation. Even for acquired SMD, Luria (1966) suggested that problems with arithmetic may arise from lesions in many different parts of the brain as well as from general impairments in brain function. This of course is consistent with his analysis of the various different operations involved in mathematics.

Where MD and RD co-occur it may be reasonable to suggest that the left hemisphere of the brain could be more involved, as language and symbolic functions may be central to the difficulties.

Siegel (1985) reported that children with SMD performed similarly to RD children on tests of *visual* short-term memory (STM) and significantly more poorly than normally reading children, but were less handicapped on *auditory* STM tasks than RD children. This provides more evidence about the handicaps that are common to *generalised or combined LDs*, as well as about the possibility that somewhat different processing problems may contribute to SMD. On the basis of his review, Geary (1993) suggests that two distinct deficits—in procedural (computational) skills, and in memory-retrieval—have different developmental pathways in SMD, with the former being delayed and subject to "catch-up" with age, and the latter being more persistent. Retrieval deficits are more commonly associated with RD and specific language problems, whereas visuo-spatial deficits are not. This latter claim is hard to reconcile with the Seigel (1985) work noted earlier, illustrating perhaps how much there is to be done in researching mathematical disabilities.

Attempts at sub-typing SMD have been made although they are limited by the scarcity of knowledge about exactly what goes wrong for children who fail in mathematical learning. Geary (1993) has argued that developmental and acquired forms of "dyscalculia" do share the same deficits, and that similar types can be extracted including "alexia" (reading problems) and "agraphia" (writing problems) for numbers, "spatial acalculia", and "anarithmetria". But the histories of the developmental and acquired forms are usually so different that such claims must be treated cautiously. Certainly there are major individual differences in patterns of deficits; whether they cohere into clear sub-types in young children is quite another question.

Postulated differential hemisphere links are complicated by the common association with RD which implicates verbal deficits and left hemisphere processes. It is argued that for children with difficulties in spatial representation of numerical information, the right hemisphere may be the site of dysfunction and where this is the primary or only difficulty, the SMD may be distinct from RD or from combined difficulties. It is unknown how many children might show this pattern. Problems particularly with memory for facts and procedures in mathematics have been linked to the left hemisphere, but these commonly overlap with RD problems. It is possible that where RD and MD co-occur there may be a common underlying deficit which is genetically based and which might involve semantic memory problems (Thompson, Detterman, & Plomin, 1991).

For those interested in SMD there is relatively little theoretical or experimental research in either cognitive or neuropsychological domains, by comparison with the wealth of material available about reading development and disabilities. This is clearly an area needing more concentrated focus of attention, no matter whether SMD is considered as closely related to RDs, or whether it is considered as a separate field for investigation. As noted earlier, behavioural genetic studies will be most profitable when there is a more comprehensive documentation of underlying processes and neuropsychological associations in carefully described and diagnosed SMD children.

NEUROPSYCHOLOGICAL TESTING

One of the hindrances to the usefulness of neuropsychology in understanding SLD has been the dearth of reliable and valid tests appropriate for use with children. Most of the measures used have been taken from the adult neuropsychology field, often with only minor modifications made to tests, to try to make them suitable for children. We do not have good evidence about the relationships between the developing brain and the processes or functions measured by adult tests, even when they have downward age extensions. Therefore using adult tests especially with young children may produce results that are difficult to interpret. For children over the age of 12 years, this problem is less serious, because a number of studies have shown that from this age, normal children's performance is likely to approximate that of adults. Nevertheless caution is warranted in comparisons of the performance of 12-year-olds with that of adults, who clearly have had much more experience in dealing with cognitive problems and challenges. This "life experience" will influence brain–behaviour relationships as assessed via neuropsychological tests.

In recent years the psychometric, if not the developmental, challenges of neuropsychological testing for children have been tackled to some extent. For some tests, there are now data on normal populations of children of different ages which allow more confidence in interpretations of individual performance. In the neuropsychological tests discussed here, the availability of normative data will be noted. In general, the younger the child the less likely we are to have a reliable and valid neuropsychological measure. Indeed it is probably safe to say that for children below the age of 8 or 9 years, there are very few suitable specific tests, and administration of the WISC-III, or the Wechsler Pre-School and Primary Scale of Intelligence–Revised (for children 3–7 years) is the most diagnostically valid and informative assessment method available.

There are some particular test batteries available for children such as the Halstead-Reitan Neuropsychological Battery, and the

Luria-Nebraska Neuropsychological Battery. These were originally developed to assist in the diagnosis of brain dysfunction in adults and have been extended down to childhood. They assess a comprehensive range of functions including: visual-spatial constructional abilities, auditory perception, tactile perception, sensorimotor integration, body image, motor functions, laterality or hemispheric differences, memory, language, academic achievement, and tactile perception. These batteries are very long, very demanding of the child, and very costly to administer. Psychometrically they provide considerable redundant information which means that the extensive time and effort in using such batteries is rarely warranted. They are unnecessary either for diagnosis, or for prescriptions for intervention in SLDs. They often provide little more useful information than can be obtained via administration of intelligence tests such as the Wechsler Scales. Equally, if not more, useful profiles of strengths and weaknesses may be obtained with more focused, neuropsychological approaches, using selected tests based on an hypothesis-testing model. Batteries also do not tap into the more detailed neurolinguistic processing problems often underlying RD. They cannot be used to throw light on localisation in the brain of any dysfunction, nor to predict outcome.

Hypothesis testing and selection of methods

Much to be preferred is the hypothesis-testing model of neuropsychological assessment which was outlined in the previous chapter, and which builds on from administration of basic screening assessment of intelligence and learning capacities. From the analysis of these screening task performances, hypotheses relating to the specific capacities thought to be problematic in the individual child can be developed. For example, consistently below-average scores on the Digit Span, Arithmetic, and Coding sub-tests from the WISC, may suggest problems with memory and concentration, which need more in-depth assessment. Low scores on Vocabulary and Similarities in a child who is struggling to read, in combination with strong performance on tests such as Block Design and Object Assembly suggest that there are language and verbal conceptual impairments which may handicap reading, in a background of good "fluid" intelligence. Hence the testing to follow might test an hypothesis of specific language weaknesses that underlie the reading and spelling problems.

Problems in remembering words in print despite many repetitions, combined with evidence of visual sequencing and memory difficulties suggest an hypothesis of visual memory impairments, which can be further assessed using specialised tests. Similarly, problems in verbal expression and articulation with immature language observed in conversation, poor comprehension of verbal material, and difficulties in word recognition and comprehension lead to an hypothesis of developmental language disorder which may best be assessed with the help of speech pathology expertise.

Having developed and tested hypotheses regarding specific impairments, the neuropsychologist would usually wish to try to move on to the next step, which is to attempt to explicate connections between both quantitative and qualitative test performance, and the localisation or extent of brain damage which influences that performance. However, this is not always appropriate or useful with SLD children, as in most cases there will be minimal evidence of brain damage, and indeed children have probably been referred for assessment in part because there is no clear organic explanation for their learning problems.

Neuropsychological test information is most profitably used in the case of SLDs in providing a picture of underlying abilities and disabilities which may be influencing the failure to learn successfully. For example, diagnosis of auditory memory impairments, or attention deficits, can lead to suggestions for methods to improve these capacities, in a way that will help more effective learning. It is unrealistic to expect a neuropsychological assessment of an SLD child to pinpoint neurological damage, and of course it can rarely be matched up to brain scan information in the way that is common in adult work, to confirm or disconfirm the hypotheses under test.

Neuropsychological tests that are useful in following up specific hypotheses

Spreen and Strauss (1991) have provided a *Compendium of neuropsychological tests* which covers most of the major measures for children. Hence only a selection of tests will be described here to illustrate the practice of neuropsychology with SLD children.

Because memory and learning are so central in mastery of the three Rs, it is not surprising that many specialised tests have been constructed to assess various aspects of these capacities.

Assessment of memory.   Almost every neuropsychological assessment undertaken will include some measures of memory. Like attention, memory is a multi-faceted ability involving not only differing modalities (visual, auditory, tactile, kinaesthetic), but different types of memory such as strategic, semantic, episodic, incidental, short-term and long-term (for review see Boyd, 1988). Memory tasks can also vary in complexity, from simple repetition of meaningless material (such as a series of numbers), to recall of meaningful material such as stories which will have required more sophisticated attentional and memory strategies. The more specific the hypothesis that is generated concerning particular types of memory deficits, and the more specific the tests designed for assessment of a particular attribute of memory, the more useful will be the information gained.

An "omnibus" test which can provide useful diagnostic information is the Wide Range Assessment of Memory and Learning (WRAML) (Sheslow & Adams, 1990), which evaluates verbal and visual memory and learning capacities. It contains a number of sub-tests grouped into verbal, visual, and learning areas, many of which are somewhat similar to other "stand-alone" tests (such as for example the Rey Auditory Verbal Learning Test). It has US norms for children from 5 to 17 years, and is argued to be able to distinguish between memory capacity and learning capacity, to identify comparative strengths in visual and verbal modalities, and to assess the extent of decay or loss of learned information. The sub-tests were constructed to permit assessment in visual and verbal modalities, to test memory for both meaningful and non-meaningful information, and to assess learning over multiple trials. These tests try to tap into a child's memory strategies over time, to include immediate, delayed, and recognition memory, and to cover the age range from childhood through adolescence.

Its authors claim that it is particularly useful in identifying the memory deficits of SLD children. WRAML scores (especially the General Memory index) correlate significantly with the Verbal, Performance, and Full Scale IQ estimates from the WISC-R but do not explain more than 35% of the variance in intelligence. The relationships between WRAML scores and Reading, Spelling, and Arithmetic scores from the WRAT are also significant but moderate in strength. At this stage it is unknown to what extent WRAML scores are more predictive of achievement in the three Rs by comparison with intelligence estimates.

Where memory deficits are hypothesised, testing with the WRAML is often a useful follow-up to the WISC and can provide a profile of individual strengths and weaknesses across the areas noted earlier. Such information can be utilised in planning intervention strategies that make the most of the child's current capacities.

The most simple and frequently used specific memory tests include a measure of Digit Span i.e. immediate memory for lists of numbers, which is part of the WISC, and also a sub-test of the ITPA. Digits backwards, from the WISC, is conventionally used as a test of "working memory", i.e. the ability to hold in memory and manipulate information in a strategic way. Memory for Sentences, which is part of the Stanford Binet Intelligence Test, and of the WRAML, assesses immediate memory for meaningful material. There are other tests of sentence memory such as that of Benton (1975). However most of these lack evidence of respectable psychometric properties so it is more useful to use the Stanford Binet sub-test which has the advantage of normative data across the age range. Story memory, which is also included in the WRAML, tests longer-term storage and understanding of meaningful prose and is probably the kind of assessment closest to everyday life tasks for the child. If a child is well below age-appropriate level on memory for meaningful material, it is not hard to see why he or she might be struggling in class to process and remember instructions from the teacher. Hence, an estimate of memory span can be used to help in recommending modifications in the amount or length of material presented, so that the child can cope with the information.

Tests of visual memory are also available including a sub-test of the ITPA, (short-term memory for a series of non-meaningful black and white visual symbols) which can be used for children up to the age of 10 or 11 years, and the Benton Visual Retention Test–Revised (1974) which also measures visuo-constructive abilities through the use of design drawing tasks.

The Rey Auditory Verbal Learning Test, measures the capacity to remember lists of unrelated words, both immediately and after a delay period. It assesses susceptibility to interference, ability for new learning, and recognition memory. There are normative data for adolescents for North America and Australia (Forrester & Geffen, 1990) and limited normative data for younger Australian children have recently been reported by Anderson, Lajoie, and Bell (1995).

The Token Test for children, which is described later in the Language section, also assesses memory for spoken instructions. It can be diagnostically and therapeutically useful in considering recommendations for classroom teaching for SLD children who have problems remembering a series of instructions.

More complex tests of memory include the Buschke Selective Reminding Test which can be used with verbal and non-verbal material, but which has only limited normative data for children (see Spreen & Strauss, 1991).

Language assessment.   A useful test of verbal fluency is the Controlled Oral Word Association Test (sometimes called Word Fluency or the FAS test). This assesses the child's ability to spontaneously generate words beginning with a given letter (e.g. F, A, or S), or a specific class of words (e.g. animals, fruit). The test is timed, in that one minute is allowed for generating words beginning with each letter. There are some normative data for school-aged children from the US and from

Australia (Spreen & Strauss, 1991). Children with impoverished vocabularies, or who are very slow to access specific words from their memory, produce few words on this test. Poor word fluency is bound to impinge on reading fluency because a child who has word-finding problems is likely to be slow to think of a probable candidate for a word in print that is unfamiliar. Children with these problems will need more time to search for words and will need more cues to "jog" their memories. They may also need intervention to help them develop more extended vocabularies.

The Token Test (di Simoni 1978) was developed to detect subtle receptive language impairments. The child is presented with an array of tokens of differing size, shape, and colour, and then is asked to perform various manipulation of these tokens. The test moves from very simple requests such as "touch the green circle", to more complex ones such as "after picking up the green square, touch the white circle". It is useful for testing hypotheses such as: (a) the child does not hear or process instructions given by the parent or teacher; (b) the child has difficulty with longer and more complicated demands (verbal memory components), and forgets what he or she is supposed to be doing; (c) the child has problems with remembering the ordering or sequence of verbal information.

Like so many children's tests that are derived from adult versions, the Token Test lacks good normative data to help in determining the extent of any handicap. However if the child shows serious difficulties with this test it suggests at the very least that modifications are necessary in the amount and kind of verbal information which should be given, and that there is need to develop strategies such as using short sentences, until the child is able to act accurately on those, before building up gradually to more complex pieces of information. SLD children with such language impairments will soon "switch off" in the classroom if they cannot process verbal instructions fast and accurately enough to be able to follow through with them.

Auditory discrimination problems which are sometimes found in children with language and learning difficulties can be tested at a simple screening level using the Wepman Auditory Discrimination Test. This is a measure of children's ability to pick up subtle differences in spoken language. Inability to do so may lead a child to develop inaccurate word storage, making it difficult for him or her to accurately perceive and remember words in print as well as in spoken language. In this test the child is asked to respond "same" or "different" to pairs of spoken words such as "tree'/ "free". Suspected serious auditory discrimination problems should of course be referred for comprehensive testing using audiology and speech pathology services.

Measures of attentional capacities.   A very common problem in SLD children is poorly regulated attention. This puts them at a severe disadvantage in structured learning situations such as the classroom. Such children may have great difficulty in maintaining concentration, in knowing when to inhibit responses, i.e. to control impulsivity, and in developing "Stop, Look, and Listen" strategies, which are necessary for good judgement and effective problem solving and decision making. Parents and teachers often provide vivid descriptions of the child's problems with attention and how this hinders effective learning. Nevertheless, not all children with these difficulties will be inattentive in a one-to-one testing session, indicating that in some situations they have the capacity to attend well.

Although there have been many attempts to develop diagnostically valid measures of attention for children, this has been a difficult task, not least because attention is not a unitary concept but involves a large number of related processes. These include focused attention (paying attention to only one critical stimulus at a time); selective attention (picking out from an array one specific target stimulus and responding only to that); sustained attention or vigilance (maintaining attention to a task over an extended period of time); as well as more central biological processes such as alertness or "arousal".

Most assessments of attentional capacities have relied on the child's performance on drawing and copying tests, along with observations during psychometric test performance (such as excessive fidgetiness), but such measures lack reliability and validity. There are several versions of a popular adaptable test, the "Continuous Performance Task" where the child has to respond over a period of time to only one type of stimulus and inhibit responses to others. For example a common form of this test is to flash letters on to a screen and have the child respond to the letter X but only after it follows the letter A. Performance on this task is usually worse in children with attention deficits (many of whom are also LD). Sanson (1984) found that in fact only children with both SLDs and reported attention problems performed poorly on this kind of task, although many clinicians use this test for diagnostic purposes in cases of suspected Attention Deficit Hyperactivity Disorder.

There are other paper and pencil tasks such as "letter cancellation" where the child has to draw a line through specifically targeted letters, trying not to miss any and not to mark non-target letters, within a specified time limit; or the Underlining Test which requires the child to underline only those stimuli that match a sample provided at the top of the page. SLD children with attention problems typically perform in a haphazard fashion on such tasks, they seem unable to develop an organised strategy such as working systematically, line by line, and checking their work.

Other tests of this genre which have been used to assess attention, impulsivity, and distractibility, include the Children's Embedded Figures Test, maze following tasks, the Matching Familiar Figures Test, and the Span of Apprehension Test. These do not have good normative data.

The Paced Auditory Serial Addition task (Gronwall & Sampson, 1974) can be used with older children to test sustained concentration and strategy deployment during a complex task. Listening to a series of regularly presented numbers, the child has to add a number to the one previously heard, offer the solution, and then go on and repeat this response with new numbers, over periods of time of varying lengths. It is a challenging task, drawing on the child's capacity for focused and sustained attention while performing quite complex cognitive operations.

The Freedom from Distractibility factor of the WISC (as noted in Chapter 4) which encompasses the three sub-tests of Arithmetic, Coding, and Digit Span can also provide a measure of attentional control, but as memory, numerical facility and adequate visuo-motor skills are also involved in these tasks, it would be an oversimplification to attribute poor scores on this factor to attention problems alone. Furthermore, some children show problems with only one or perhaps two of these sub-tests and may do quite well on the other.

Systematic observations in the classroom of a child's "off-task" and "on-task" behaviour have also been used to assess attention problems in more naturalistic settings, in children with Attention Deficit Hyperactivity Disorder and SLDs. However, as with so many tests in this domain, there is little normative data, making it difficult to tell whether a child has problems that go beyond the normal range of individual differences in attentional processes. Nevertheless it is important to consider this aspect of everyday behaviour in assessing attention in SLD children, because it is such a powerful influence on the ability to learn effectively in the classroom.

Many children with serious attention problems as reported by parents and teachers will be able to work well and in a sustained fashion when being assessed by a professional in a distraction-free environment. With firm structure imposed by systematic task application, and a high level of motivation to perform well for an authority figure, some children seem to be able to overcome fidgetiness and problems with concentration, at least temporarily. The positive aspect of this kind of experience is that it demonstrates that in some situations the child with attention difficulties is able to exercise control, and that he or she has the capacity to sustain attention. This has implications for the way in which well-regulated classroom management techniques can be put in place to assist a child with problems in controlling attention.

However it is also true that once the child becomes more habituated to any situation his or her usual attention deficits are likely to emerge, so the professional should be wary of assuming that the deficits are not real ones on the basis of behaviour in the clinical or assessment setting.

Successful intervention to manage the attentional difficulties can lead to substantial gains in children's performance on academic tasks, hence careful assessment of these capacities is extremely important.

Visual/perceptual problems.   The Beery Developmental Test of Visual Motor Integration (VMI; Beery, 1967) assesses visual–motor integration in children from 4 to 15 years of age. The task is to copy geometric forms which are presented in order of increasing difficulty. It is a similar test to the Bender Gestalt Test which has been very popular in the assessment of children for many years. However, like the Bender, the Beery requires some subjectivity in scoring the accuracy of the copies, and in interpreting the meaning of observed difficulties. But it does serve as a measure of the child's developmental level of perceptual motor skills and may have some relevance in the understanding of some aspects of LDs, especially skill in copying letters and words and in remembering the "look" of a word to be read or spelled.

The Benton Test of Visual Retention was noted earlier under Memory. It provides assessment of visual perception and visuo-constructive abilities as well as visual memory.

The Rey–Osterrieth Complex Figure Test (Rey Figure) assesses visuospatial constructional ability and visual memory, as well as planning and organisational skills. The child is asked to copy a complex figure which has a number of distinct sections. As the child completes each section of the drawing he or she is given a different coloured pencil, and the tester notes the order of colour use so that the organisation of the copy can be tracked.

Total time to complete the drawing is noted and this should be no more than five minutes. After an interval of time, which can be up to 30 minutes (delayed recall) the child, without prior warning, is asked to reproduce the drawing from memory. Detailed scoring criteria are provided (Spreen & Strauss, 1991), and norms for children are now available, although care should be taken to ensure that the test instructions are consistent with those used in the normative sample, as there has been some variation in the ways in which the test has been administered and scored. Visuo-constructive memory problems can often be revealed in this test which may relate to a child's problems with remembering words and numerical symbols. Attentional and organisational deficits will also be evident in children who rush at the task and produce inaccurate, chaotic copies which show no sense of strategy use.

Other concept formation and problem-solving measures.   Some children have difficulty in forming concepts (as shown for example by poor performance on the Similarities sub-test of the WISC-III); in hypothesis development and testing; discovering and adhering to strategies or principles; or alternatively, in the ability to be flexible, i.e. to shift set or change principles when required. A number of neuropsychological tests are available which focus on these capacities, including the Category Test, Raven's Progressive Matrices, and the Wisconsin Card Sorting Test.

The Category Test which is a sub-test from the Halstead Reitan Battery is designed to assess higher-order concept formation or abstraction ability and problem-solving skills. The child is visually presented with sets of items which are organised according to a particular principle or rule, e.g. number, ordinal position, odd one out, etc. The child is not given any rules but must develop the principle of categorisation based on feedback given for correct or incorrect responses. Performance is related to non-verbal intelligence and does not show any relationship with specific location of brain damage. It is useful for measuring a child's ability to generate and test hypotheses, to learn concepts and categories, and to make use of corrective feedback to change strategies when needed.

Raven's Progressive Matrices is a well-known test involving visual reasoning in which the child has to find a missing piece to complete a pattern, or to decide between alternatives which one best fits a pattern. The test is supposed to not require verbalisation, manipulation ability, or subtle analysis of visual information. However some research has shown that, not surprisingly, children do help themselves by at least covertly developing verbal instructions, descriptions, and categories. It is most commonly used as a test of "g" or general intelligence, but there is some evidence that it taps into right hemisphere abilities and it is a useful measure of abstraction ability. Norms are available although they may be somewhat out of date. The qualitative data gleaned from watching and analysing how a child goes about solving the problems are also useful in neuropsychological assessment.

The Wisconsin Card Sorting Test has been popular in neuro-psychological work and is believed to be related to frontal lobe functioning, in that it assesses the ability to form abstract concepts and to be flexible in maintaining and shifting set while problem solving. The task for the child is to sort cards into categories (not specified by the examiner, hence to be guessed at). The child is told when he or she is right or wrong and has to use this feedback to try to get as many cards right as possible.

Performance is scored according to the number of correct categories achieved, the number of "perseverative responses", i.e. when the child fails to change set and persists with a previously correct but now incorrect response; and a learning ability index which reflects changes in efficiency across trials. Limited normative data are available for children, although again, because scoring methods are somewhat variable, the tester needs to ensure that his or her methods are consistent with those used in the comparison sample. The "best" measure is thought to be perseverative errors which are claimed to reflect frontal lobe damage. For SLD children, the qualitative data obtained through these measures of strategy development and use are of most value in understanding cognitive limitations and how they might impinge on academic progress and the ability to profit by classroom instruction.

Solving mazes such as the Milner Maze task (Spreen & Strauss, 1991) can also provide information on a child's planning and organisational capacities and the ability to remember and profit from feedback about errors.

SUMMARY

In summary, advances in neuropsychological theory and practice over the past two or three decades have been helpful in the development of assessment methods which can be used in gaining more detailed and in-depth understanding of some of the cognitive difficulties that characterise LD children. Neuropsychology is still very much a developing "science" and its ability to underpin confident assertions about brain-behaviour relationships is limited. For SLD children and their teachers, its value in describing and explaining cognitive processes, and in guiding prescriptions for remedial treatment and more adaptive learning strategies, depends very much on the skill of the neuropsychologist in communicating the nature and significance of the connections uncovered through assessment.

This chapter concludes with an example of how neuropsychological assessment can help in understanding the complex cognitive difficulties experienced by an SLD child and how it can be used to devise a learning programme to facilitate academic progress.

ILLUSTRATIVE CASE HISTORY

Jane was 12½ years old, and in the first year of secondary school when she was brought for assessment because of persisting difficulties in reading and spelling. She suffers from eczema and asthma, and before she began school she sustained a mild head injury twice. Neither occasion resulted in any loss of consciousness. Her academic difficulties were first observed in Grade 1 and by Grade 4 they had become of serious concern. Private tutoring for two years was helpful but did not overcome her literacy problems which are now hampering her in all subjects in the secondary school curriculum. Jane's social relationships appear adequate and she has areas of strength in gymnastics, basketball, and mathematics. She uses her left hand for writing, her left foot for kicking, and throws and catches with her right hand. Vision and hearing have tested normal.

Testing with the WISC III, and the Wide Range Achievement Test showed that Jane was at a low average level of intellectual ability with no difference between verbal and performance IQ. She was reading at about a Grade 3 level and was very slow. Spelling was even further below at about a 7-year-old level. She showed evidence of some phonological skills.

Jane's greatest strengths were in completing mazes, which taps planning ability, perceptual organisation and visuo-motor control; Digit Span, (short-term auditory memory), and in Similarities (conceptual reasoning). Arithmetic, Block Design, and Object Assembly sub-tests were all in the normal range.

Specific problems uncovered by these tests included a very limited store of vocabulary knowledge and general information, (probably influenced at this stage by years of limited access to written material), and visuo-spatial weaknesses in tasks that required rapid shifts of attention, sequential processing, and scanning under time pressure.

Several hypotheses were considered:

a)   Jane had problems with sequencing material as evidenced by her problems with Coding, Picture Arrangement, and Symbol Search sub-tests of the WISC.

b)   She had difficulties with speed of information processing as shown by inability to work at speed on the Coding sub-test, extremely slow word recognition, and a very slow style with most tasks.

c)   Memory consolidation was weak, as even though she could learn associations she forgot them shortly afterwards.

d)   Jane had a visual scanning problem which would hamper her on the Picture Completion sub-test (finding missing detail from a picture—where she was a little below average), and the Picture Arrangement and the Coding sub-tests which were notably poor. Jane was also observed to sometimes turn or move the page she was working on, rather than using her head and eyes for scanning.

These hypotheses were tested in the following ways: The Wide Range Assessment of Memory and Learning showed that Jane was very poor on Sentence Memory, and on the Sound Symbol Test (which requires learning associations between sound and visual symbols, a capacity that seems to relate closely to reading ability), and below average on Picture Memory, and Finger Windows (a sequential visual memory test). Her visual memory was a little better than her verbal memory and there were relative strengths in memory for stories and for designs. Her poorest sub-tests on the WRAML were those involving the ability to remember sequences in both modalities. Although Jane showed an adequate learning curve for verbal auditory material, her memory was very poor after a delay period. Timed tasks involving memory for symbols and sequences were most difficult for her and her slow speed of information processing was a major hindrance.

In addition, she was given the Trail Making Test from the Reitan Battery which measures sequential ability by requiring the child to connect a series of letters and numbers in alternating order. Jane made no errors on this test but was so slow that she was well outside the normative score range. It seemed that there was evidence supporting the hypotheses of sequencing difficulties from a number of sources. These tests also supported the proposition that speed of information processing was a problem.

Testing of her memory produced mixed results. Her overall memory score was towards the low end of average and consistent with her WISC IQ. Looking at the various aspects of memory that were tested, showed that Jane was very good on memory for designs and for stories read to her, but as noted earlier, picture and sentence memory and visual sequences were below average. It was also notable that her retention after a delay period was poor. However, her drawing of the Complex Figure of Rey and her score on reproduction of the figure after a 30-minute delay was average. On some spontaneous tests of long-term memory, such as naming the location of a hidden object two hours after the hiding event and remembering what her Christmas presents had been, Jane had no difficulties. This was also the case for delayed recall of the details of a story and learning of word lists (from the WRAML). The long-term memory deficit hypothesis appeared not to be confirmed.

The visual scanning hypothesis was assessed using the letter cancellation task and here Jane was perfectly able to perceive and discriminate the target letters, even though she moved the page rather than her head in working through the material. It is possible that she may have difficulty in copying work from the classroom blackboard which she is, of course, unable to move. It is likely that this is a "style of work" she has developed rather than a neuropsychological problem.

Overall, it appeared from this rather mixed and complex neuropsychological picture that the major difficulties were evident when sequencing of material was required, and that Jane had difficulty in both speed and accuracy, particularly in sequencing visual material. Conceptual material was not exempt from this problem, as shown in the low Picture Arrangement score. Any problems with memory may be related to her sequencing difficulties, because in general she did not show generalised deficits, with either verbal or visual material.

The poor score on sentence memory is hard to explain but may be due to a lapse of concentration during a rote task of minimal interest to her. Although she is a relatively slow processor, this weakness was not evident on all timed tests, only those involving visual sequencing of material. Her strengths lie in tasks that involve reasoning and problem solving in both verbal and visual modalities. Her motivation, attention, and concentration were good throughout the quite lengthy assessment sessions.

Most of the evidence points to sequencing problems especially at speed, and this is relevant to Jane's slow progress with reading where she has to remember sequences of letters and words to achieve word recognition and sentence meaning, and then to consolidate this in long-term memory. A neuropsychological interpretation would implicate left hemisphere processing as being impaired on the basis of the sequential processing difficulties and the poor vocabulary and reading skills. But the picture was not a clear one as Jane has some strengths in some verbal domains.

The connections between the neuropsychological testing and reading and spelling difficulties appear complex. Difficulties that were uncovered in learning associations between visual and auditory symbols will almost certainly impinge on reading skills, and Jane's problems in remembering sequences in either visual or verbal forms will add to the challenge. The complex multiple symbolic associations and sequences at the word and sentence level required for reading are very difficult for this girl.

Recommendations for intervention included repeated practice with new words to improve Jane's immediate word-recognition vocabulary, and reinforcing the use of her phonological skills in attacking new words that are regular in their characteristics. Together these strategies can rapidly build up a larger vocabulary which can assist with comprehension and speed of reading.

Use of a Talking Book approach (i.e. repetitive reading of the same passages with the help of an audiotaped model) to improve fluency and speed in reading, was recommended on a trial basis. Reading and spelling tasks need to be small-scale and easily achievable at first to enhance Jane's confidence and experience of success. Her teachers should be made aware of her sequencing problems and should adjust their instructions and requirements to take account of this fact. Repeated opportunities to use and rehearse language skills and to expand her vocabulary and store of general knowledge need to be provided. Jane's efforts should be given abundant praise and her existing strengths emphasised in the overall programme.

CHAPTER SIX

The relationship between behaviour problems and learning difficulties

INTRODUCTION

It has long been known that learning problems and behaviour problems tend to go together. That is, children who have SLDs are more likely than non-SLD children to have behavioural and emotional problems (BPs) of one sort or another; and children with behavioural and emotional problems are likely to be at high risk for the development of SLDs. The overlap between behaviour problems and learning disabilities is usually found to be about 40 or 50% depending on which kinds of problems are considered. The association is high for the disorder popularly known as "Hyperactivity". This is currently classified as a disorder called "Attention Deficit Hyperactivity Disorder" (ADHD) and it is clearly associated with SLDs from the earliest school years. Conduct Disorder and anti-social behaviour are also strongly associated with SLDs. These SLD–BP relationships hold especially strongly for boys.

Girls are much less prone to behaviour problems of the disruptive type, and even if they are SLD, they are less likely to be troublesome and hard to manage in class, compared with SLD boys.

The association between SLDs and BPs is of great significance over the long term, as both behaviour problems and academic problems are likely to persist, and both are related to maladjustment, social deviance, unemployment, and unhappiness in later life.

Hence many SLD children are doubly disadvantaged; they and their parents and teachers have two sets of problems to contend with. It also means that both sets of problems need to be treated, if the child is to avoid a very poor long-term outcome. The relationship between childhood BPs and long-term psychosocial disadvantage including delinquency, unemployment, and unstable and unhappy interpersonal relationships is well documented (Rutter & Giller, 1983). This outcome may be considerably worsened if the individual is also SLD. In fact, much research shows that it is the influence of associated BPs, rather than "pure" SLDs, which plays the major role in a poor adult outcome. Thus this is a very important area of consideration for those working with SLD (and behaviour-disordered) children.

If a child's cognitive and emotional energy is directed towards disruptive behaviour, or if he or she is preoccupied with feelings of sadness and failure, there may be little attention and motivation left for the process of learning. Even well-directed remedial efforts can fail if the child's emotional and behavioural state is not taken into account.

ILLUSTRATIVE CASE HISTORY

The following illustrates a typical case of a boy with multiple problems of learning and behaviour, who met criteria for SLD.

Simon was referred for assessment at the age of 12 years by a Special Education Assistant at his secondary school. He has had longstanding difficulties at school both academically and in his behaviour. His teachers find him disruptive in class and he rarely completes set work assignments. He is receiving some remedial help and has also been provided with a behaviour modification programme based on a point system, to assist him to stay on task.

Simon's WISC-R IQ is 100, with his verbal IQ being 92 and his performance IQ 109. His reading, spelling, and arithmetic were all four or five years behind grade level, with his arithmetic marginally better than reading and spelling. His reading comprehension was two years ahead of his accuracy, indicating that he could use his intelligence to make sense of printed material despite being unable to read accurately.

Neuropsychological testing showed that Simon had memory problems in both auditory and visual modalities but could do relatively well if the material to be learned was structured and organised for him.

His own organisation of new information was poor and he did not monitor his performance very well. On none of the memory tests was Simon in the normal or expected range for his age. However it was notable that his attention and concentration were very fluctuating and this may have influenced his variable performance on tests relying on organisation and memory.

Teacher reports emphasised Simon's problems with concentration and organisation, his continual talking and disrupting other children, his social immaturity leading to some rejection by other children (although he has a group of friends with similar problems), and a collection of attention deficit/hyperactivity disorder symptoms including fidgeting, distractibility, restlessness, impulsivity, short attention span, attention-getting behaviour, and being "anxious to please". One teacher raised the possibility that Simon had "Attention Deficit Disorder with Hyperactivity". Despite a high level of care and concern by the school, with provision of special assistance on a regular basis, Simon was a very long way behind the remainder of children in his class and the gap seemed almost insurmountable, given that he was now 12. His behavioural difficulties were clearly interfering with his ability to learn and to profit by the extra help he was given.

Recommendations made on the basis of the assessment included: continuing one-to-one remedial assistance, with some specific suggestions for phonics training in reading, and a multi-sensory approach to learning to spell accurately, (repeated practice of oral and written spelling with routine visual checking); reassuring Simon that he is not "dumb" (this was his description of himself), and pointing out his positive attributes such as his willingness to keep trying, and his sporting abilities; a comprehensive behaviour management programme focused on classroom behaviour problems, including impulsivity, calling out in class, completing homework, and concentrating on his work programme.

It was also suggested that he could be enrolled in a special structured day programme provided by a local Adolescent Mental Health Service, especially designed for young adolescents, and aimed at improving social behaviour and interpersonal interaction skills. Simon's mother, who found her son very hard to manage, was referred to a local community support and counselling service where it was hoped she would receive help in providing a supportive and disciplined home environment for him, and in coping with her own worries and disappointments in the face of Simon's long history of difficulties.

"EXTERNALISING" BEHAVIOUR PROBLEMS

The kinds of BPs most closely associated with SLDs are thought to be the "acting out", "undercontrolled", or "externalising" disorders, so called because they consist of behaviours that bring the child into conflict with the external environment and the people in it. Behaviours in the externalising cluster encompass defiant, aggressive, disruptive, impulsive, and antisocial acts including fighting, bullying, temper outbursts, disobedience, and uncooperative behaviour. These patterns may be present at home and in the school environment, and they lead to the child being negatively perceived by all around him or her. They present serious difficulties in management for caretakers. Children with severe behavioural difficulties of the externalising type are given various diagnostic labels, including Conduct Disorder, Oppositional Defiant Disorder, and Antisocial Disorder. The prevalence of these kinds of BPs is *estimated* at about 9% for boys and 2% for girls.

Such behaviour problems are somewhat more common in economically disadvantaged, lower social class groups, and in families where there is conflict and where nurture, supervision, and discipline are not always adequate for healthy development. Hence disadvantage is piled upon disadvantage with family, social, psychological, and behavioural factors combining to put such children at very high risk for SLDs.

An externalising disorder that is strongly associated with SLDs is that collection of behaviours which comprise the disorder known as "Attention Deficit Hyperactivity Disorder" (ADHD). The behaviours in this disorder include short attention span, difficulties in concentrating, distractibility, poor impulse control, failure to finish anything undertaken, losing things at school, difficulty sitting still, calling out in class, poor planning and organisational abilities, and unregulated activity patterns, which may be expressed in overactivity, and/or purposeless activity. Estimates of the prevalence of ADHD vary considerably but these children are probably about 3% to 5% of the population. Boys outnumber girls by about 4 to 1 according to most published studies, although McGee and Feehan (1991) have argued that girls with problems of attention are under-recognised and that the male predominance may be an artefact of selection criteria for children in research studies. They found no differences between ADHD boys and girls in type or severity of any behaviours, or attributes associated with the disorder, in their New Zealand sample.

Some researchers have argued that the associations between SLDs and BPs are primarily in this domain. It is the ADHD child who is most at risk for SLD in the early years of schooling, with an overlap in disorders of 40% to 50%. However there is also evidence of a strong association with Conduct or Antisocial Disorder, and in fact all kinds of psychological disorders are represented in the SLD population.

The associations with Conduct Disorder or externalising behaviour problems may come via the association between ADHD and conduct problems, as these frequently co-occur. The most severely affected children have a combination of ADHD, and antisocial behaviour along with academic difficulties.

Attentional and emotional problems are often reported in SMD children. Shalev et al. (1995) looked specifically at associations between attentional and anxiety problems in an SMD group (17% of whom were also RD) by comparison with normal and clinical (non-LD) control groups. Both boys and girls had significantly more attentional problems than non-SMD children but less than those of clinically referred children. SMD girls differed little from normal children on behaviour problems overall, thus mirroring findings in the RD field. Attentional difficulties were likely to be accompanied by higher levels of anxiety and depression. Overall, the percentage of MD children showing clinically significant levels of behaviour disorder was 2.5 to 3 times higher than that found in normal children, and the relationships were particularly substantial for attentional, social, and withdrawal symptoms.

ADHD symptoms are also associated with "school readiness' problems in young children even before they begin formal instruction. The immature and poorly regulated or non "rule-governed" behaviour of pre-school children with ADHD-type behaviours makes them ill-equipped to cope with the demands for control, concentration, and regulated behaviour when they arrive in the school classroom. They are not ready or able to adapt and to learn at the expected rate for their age. This makes them extremely vulnerable to escalating problems unless they are very firmly managed with a high level of authority, structure, and discipline provided by teachers and parents. They are very demanding for teachers, and in a class of 25 or more children the teacher is hard-put to cope with the disruption they cause to the class programmes. These early school readiness problems appear to be more common in boys and may be associated with the somewhat slower maturation rate for young boys, perhaps especially in capacities for language and self-regulation (Prior, Smart, Sanson, & Oberklaid, 1993).

Others, however, have argued strongly that it is the entire cluster of externalising problems, not just ADHD, that is associated with underachievement and SLDs. Problems with making clear and reliable diagnoses, as well as varying diagnostic practices in different countries and cultures, contribute to the problems in making assertions about what is the true picture here. For example, the diagnosis of ADHD is less common in Britain compared with the US; and British clinicians may be more likely to see the antisocial symptoms as primary, whereas US clinicians may focus more on ADHD symptoms. A child with similar behaviour problems may receive a different "label" depending on the country in which he or she lives. Although many children have a combination of antisocial/aggressive and ADHD problems, it is possible to find pure syndromes of each kind of disorder, and it is only relatively recently that researchers have tried to separate out the various symptom patterns to investigate more specific associations with SLDs.

It is likely that, to some extent, the relationship between BPs and SLDs is mediated by the neurocognitive deficits that are often found in these children. For example, poor language skills which hinder the child's ability to think and reason about social relationships and interpersonal conflicts, and to communicate effectively with those around him or her, may also underlie difficulties in learning to read and to spell, and to solve all types of problems. Some longitudinal studies have shown links between early language deficits and externalising BPs in adolescence, demonstrating the long-term influence of language factors.

In looking at these relationships, we are faced again with the "what comes first" question, because any deficits found on formal cognitive or language assessment may be a *consequence* of SLDs which may have slowed the rate of learning and consequently the ability to do well on some types of cognitive tests that depend on learning and experience. Only prospective studies that find neurocognitive deficits which *predate* the development of SLDs and BPs, and then follow children over time to assess their progress, can speak adequately to this question.

Externalising BPs tend to persist over time and are quite difficult to modify once well established (Kazdin, 1987). They are associated with a diagnosis of "Conduct Disorder" as noted earlier, which involves persistent patterns of rule breaking, antisocial and sometimes violent behaviour, and with juvenile delinquency if children move into the domain of official law breaking.

Such behaviours are obviously not compatible with effective learning. Truanting, or illegal absence from school, which is also associated with antisocial behaviours can lead to even more disadvantage in learning, as the child or adolescent falls further and further behind the class work programmes. The presence of BPs (especially the ADHD type), is also sometimes associated with a lower than average IQ, further disadvantaging the child in learning.

"INTERNALISING" PROBLEMS

Another collection of behaviour problems about which we know rather less in the SLD field concerns "internalising", "overcontrolled" disorders or emotional problems. These include socially withdrawn behaviour, anxiety, fearfulness, and sadness or depression. These problems are much less often recognised because of their internalised nature, as they cause trouble *within* the individual rather than *between the individual and his or her social world*. Hence teachers and parents are not always fully aware that the child is suffering. Girls are rather more prone to internalise their problems, and many SLD girls may be quiet and well behaved in the classroom and their learning difficulties attract less attention. However it is also common to find boys with internalising disorders in the primary school years, or a combination of externalising and internalising symptoms.

There is good reason to suspect that there *appear* to be more SLD boys than girls because it is the boys who attract attention by their troublesome behaviours, while the girls are quiet and well behaved (Prior et al, 1995; Vogel, 1990). We know relatively little on this topic about girls because research has focused so substantially on SLDs and BPs in boys. Some of the work from the Dunedin longitudinal study of New Zealand children confirms that reading-disabled girls are often under-recognised and under-reported (McGee & Feehan, 1991).

Whatever the "true" origins and nature of the links between SLDs and BPs, the likely effects on children daily experiencing failure in school cannot be over-emphasised. SLD children are frequently criticised and denigrated by teachers and parents, and they may be rejected by peers, who are quick to perceive who stands out in the class as being unable to read and spell. As they fall further and further behind, they develop a picture of themselves as deficient, different, hopeless, and unsuccessful, unless special steps are taken to attend to these issues. Self-esteem, which is normally quite high and robust in young children, rapidly ebbs away, and SLD children lose confidence in themselves not only as students but as people who have some value in the world. Hence life at school may be a dispiriting experience and the secondary consequences of learning failure can outweigh all other experiences for the SLD child. Many teachers see the loss of confidence and self-esteem as the major challenge in trying to help SLD children.

Continuing failure and increasing distress further reduce motivation to try, and a syndrome of "learned helplessness" may produce indifference to learning, or in some cases, energetic avoidance of school work. Hence it is essential that every child should not only receive help with his or her problems in learning and in behaviour, but that areas of strength and success should be emphasised, so that at least in some areas of life the child can see himself or herself as a winner, not a loser.

TIMING OF INTERVENTIONS

How should we intervene to help children who have the combination of BPS and SLDs? The answer to this challenge, in part requires an attempt to answer the question of "what leads to what"? What are the alternative hypotheses?

- Do children with behavioural difficulties fail to learn properly because of their hyperactivity, inattention, and non-compliant behaviour?
- Or do children who fail in school during the early learning stages, develop emotional and behavioural difficulties as a reaction to their failure, hence worsening their chances of succeeding in school?
- Or is this association caused by some other factor such as developmental language problems, neurodevelopmental problems, low IQ, family social disadvantage, family conflict, or other kinds of psychosocial difficulties?
- Or do both sets of problems lead to each other, i.e. is the association *bi-directional*?

These questions have been considered by a number of researchers, with no generally agreed answer emerging from their studies. The only way to adequately understand the relationships is to take a longitudinal approach, i.e. to study the same children from early in development, across time, so that it is possible to track the emergence of the various problems as they develop. To look at only one point in time will tell you about the association but not about its origins.

Recent longitudinal studies from New Zealand (Fergusson & Horwood, 1995; Williams & McGee, 1994), Canada (Links, Boyle, & Offord, 1989); the USA (Frick et al., 1991); and from Australia (Prior et al., 1995) have looked specifically at this question (see Hinshaw, 1992, for review of literature on this topic). Results from the Australian study are informative for several reasons. First, the sample of children was from a normal population representing a whole state (Victoria), and hence was not contaminated by clinical referral biases. This is an important issue, because often the most troublesome boys are referred for treatment and less problematic girls may not be counted. Thus studies may be based on highly selected clinical groups which may not represent the picture for the general population of children.

Second, the sample was a large one including almost equal numbers of boys and girls and representing all social classes. Third, the children and their families had been studied since the children were in the first year of life, so there was a large bank of data on their early development which could show whether they had early behavioural difficulties, or indeed any other kinds of predictors of later adjustment status. Fourth, the children were followed up through the school years, with regular reports on their academic progress at school, and on their behavioural adjustment. These were provided by parents and grade teachers at two-year intervals. In Grade 2 and in Grade 6, they were administered a reading test by their grade teachers which gave a measure of their reading ability by comparison with the expected levels in a normal population.

The children in Grade 2 who were found to be reading-disabled (i.e. who were more than one standard deviation below the reading-skill level of the rest of the sample) were selected for a study of the relationship between SLDs and BPs. For these children it was possible to go back over their developmental histories to see whether they had problems at the time they entered school, and even earlier; or whether they began to develop behavioural difficulties after they experienced learning failure.

The expected strong association between SLDs and BPs, particularly for boys, was found. (In this study reading problems were the primary basis for subject selection, but the RD children had even greater difficulties in spelling, and many of them also had problems with maths.) Of those boys who were experiencing reading failure, 70% also had BPs. For the girls with RD, 50% had BPs. Both externalising and internalising behaviour problems were found in these children. Some children had internalising and externalising problems combined and those with symptoms of more than one kind of disorder were especially prone to SLDs. Teachers' ratings also showed the RD children to be poorer on a variety of specific academic and linguistic skills as judged by their classroom performance.

Several findings of this study are of particular significance in assessing the nature of the association between BPs and RDs. Follow-up of these children in Grade 4 showed that many children who had BPs in Grade 2, but who were reading well, no longer had their behavioural difficulties two years later; i.e. good academic progress was a "protective factor" in diminishing behavioural adjustment problems. The children with the combined SLD and BP problems continued to be very handicapped in both areas; they did not "grow out of" their problems as teachers sometimes claim will happen.

The developmental histories of these children showed clear evidence of behaviour problems from toddlerhood onwards, for those children who were both RD and BP. Thus, the behavioural disturbance preceded and contributed to the risk for RD. This doubly handicapped group had begun school with a combination of attention problems and poorly regulated and undercontrolled behaviour. They then went on to develop SLDs.

For children who had only RDs, i.e. no BPs, there were no indications in their early histories of the SLDs that were to come. The likelihood of SLDs could not have been predicted for the group of children with no current behaviour disorder. However it is possible that the predictors of pure reading difficulties were more "cognitive" in nature, such as early language deficiencies. Intelligence level was strongly related to poor reading, so it is clear that there are other factors which contribute to the development of SLDs in the early years of school. The higher the intelligence the lower the chance that RDs will develop. But high IQ is not a sufficient protection against RDs, nor did low IQ mean that they were inevitable.

Further follow-up into the final year of primary school for these children showed that a majority of them had not reached age-appropriate levels in their literacy skills, so the SLDs were persistent.

Many other studies have shown that behaviour problems especially of the hyperactivity and attention deficit type in kindergarten and early primary school are very consistent correlates of learning problems (e.g. Frick et al., 1991). Such general findings suggest that it would be worthwhile to focus a good deal of attention on BPs at pre-school level, and to intervene with behavioural programmes at this stage of development, to try to reduce the numbers of children (boys particularly) who are entering school with a set of behaviours that will put them at risk for learning failure. This will not eliminate SLDs, but it may substantially reduce a primary risk factor for the LD/BP combination, especially for young boys.

Low socio-economic status (SES) and family adversity are associated with an increased risk for both sets of problems. However when SES is looked at as just one aspect of the various influences on SLDs, it accounts for very little of the relationship. It is also likely that SES is a very crude measure and that nested within the SES variables are more significant and direct influences such as parental values about education, their availability and willingness to read to the child and to take an interest in his or her reading and learning progress. In addition, more specific and powerful variables including parental hostility and conflict both between parents, and from parent to child, may increase the chances for child maladjustment in behavioural and learning spheres.

Family adversity can contribute not only to the risk for BPs and SLDs, but also to the chances of recovery, with higher SES families perhaps able to garner more resources to help their children towards improved longer-term outcomes. A proportion of children with SLDs will come from families with histories of educational underachievement and cognitive/language problems. Such problems are also more common in siblings of SLD children, especially if behavioural problems are present as well. These children will need extra teaching resources if they are to have a chance of succeeding at school.

Cognitive, speech, and language delay and difficulties are also associated with risk for both behavioural and learning problems, especially ADHD, although they are insufficient on their own to provide a complete explanation for the association. They can contribute to the development of BPs, in that deficient verbal mediation skills may predispose individuals to conflictual interpersonal relationships and poor ability to think and reason about difficulties and to regulate behaviour in accordance to the demands of society. Speech and language problems provide good candidates as explanations for underlying factors in both disorders, and of the link between them.

Canadian, British, and New Zealand studies (see e.g. Spreen, 1988) have found that a variety of early neurodevelopmental risk factors, of which developmental language handicaps are only one, contribute to outcome for ADHD and SLD children.

It is clearly the case that a complex interacting set of variables encompassing behavioural, cognitive, neurodevelopmental, and psychosocial influences combine in different ways, in different children, to increase their risk for SLDs. Hence all of the variables mentioned will play a role without any one of them necessarily being the explanation of the problems.

More specific material about how to help SLD/BP children will be provided in the next chapter, but both sets of problems require intensive intervention. It is not enough to just remediate the SLDs, as the BPs will not necessarily disappear as a consequence, particularly if they are well entrenched. Similarly, behavioural programmes, no matter how successful in improving behavioural self-control, cannot be expected to completely overcome the SLDs.

On the basis of current evidence which clearly identifies BPs as risk factors and precursors to SLDs in a substantial proportion of cases, intervention in this sphere will need to be early in the child's life, i.e. to have a preventive focus for greatest effectiveness. This will need to be a joint effort, with families and kindergarten teachers involved in helping the child towards an appropriate level of readiness for learning. A major focus should be on the learning of "self-regulation", attentional, and verbal mediation skills, as it is particularly these capacities that impinge on the child's academic and social learning.

At the same time, good preparation for later learning can be provided in pre-school or day care and especially in the home. Reading, and sharing picture and story books with a child can begin at a very early age. It is a rare child who does not enjoy reading time with a parent, and if this is regular and enjoyable for both parties it can become a daily pleasure. Bedtime stories not only soothe a child ready for sleep but are an important source of language enrichment and knowledge. There is evidence that knowledge of rhymes in language is a helpful precursor to reading. Poetry and songs, nursery rhymes and books such as the Dr Seuss type "Cat in the Hat" material is educative as well as fun. Parents who talk to and read to their children are setting the scene for fostering academic competence later on. This should never be forced however; some children (and parents) can only enjoy brief "doses" of book sharing and it should never become a painful chore.

Most good pre-school programmes provide word games, singing, rhymes, and language and drama activities. These are also excellent preparation for the more serious stuff in the primary school classroom.

Pre-school teachers are very important agents in identifying children who are delayed in their language and/or social development, who are "dysregulated", non-compliant, or very troubled in their behaviour. Teacher consultation with parents and professionals about developmental difficulties, with referral for special help where necessary, is much to be preferred to letting problems drift on or become entrenched, so that the child begins school at considerable risk for behaviour and learning problems.

SUMMARY

SLDs and BPs are strongly associated and the combination of problems carries a high risk of a poor long-term outcome. The connections are more common in boys and are most likely to involve attentional problems, poor self-regulation skills and disruptive, sometimes aggressive, behaviour. Early intervention is essential to reduce the numbers of children entering school poorly equipped to succeed in mastering early learning.

CHAPTER SEVEN

Intervention

There is no definitive answer to the question of *when* a child qualifies for a diagnosis of SLD. But it is obviously better to step in with intervention strategies during the early grades rather than wait until the child is almost on the point of completing primary school with a non-functional level of academic skills, before deciding that there is a real problem. Unfortunately this latter scenario is a common one; many children in schools can be left to struggle for years with their SLDs neglected.

It is critical to find the optimum time and the right focus for intervention to decrease the chances of a poor outcome for the child at risk for SLDs. On the basis of the material presented in preceding chapters, some obvious questions to be considered are:

- Should intervention be targeted primarily at behaviour problems especially attention deficits and hyperactivity in the early pre-school years to reduce the risk for SLDs?
- Should intervention be focused on early cognitive and language capacities?
- Should increasing *parent* education about, and involvement with these children's learning be the major focus so that children are given a good start to prepare them for formal learning; or,
- Should one try to address all of these problems when they co-exist?

Alternatively, one could wait until the child has settled at school, has completed two or three years of instruction, and then assess and treat specific difficulties identified in children who are falling behind the rest of the class.

Although there is no definitive answer to the "what comes first" and the "what should be tackled first" questions posed in this volume, much of the evidence at this stage leans towards the aetiological importance of early behavioural problems in the development of learning difficulties, particularly for boys. In addition, the research supporting the importance of early language factors, especially phonemic awareness, for RD and for spelling competence, argues for a focus on these "readiness" factors in the early years, perhaps even before the child enters school.

Parents whose children show extremes of hyperactive, distractible, and poorly regulated behaviour which is clearly creating management and learning problems in the early years are well advised to seek professional help from a behavioural paediatrician or child psychologist. Concerns about slow or deviant language development should be taken seriously. It is far better to seek an early referral to a speech pathologist to have language development assessed and assisted if this is thought necessary, even at the risk of a "false positive", i.e. assessment shows that the child was mistakenly believed to be at risk.

Early intervention may not by itself solve all problems. Most "at risk" children will need ongoing monitoring, highly structured, carefully graded, and predictable classroom programmes, and continual vigilance and care on the part of parents to ensure that the child is coping well socially and academically.

Where there are signs of poor school adjustment, extreme slowness in grasping the early stages of reading, writing, and arithmetic, it is essential that the child's progress is systematically monitored and he or she is not left to struggle unaided in the hope that things will right themselves.

TREATING BEHAVIOUR PROBLEMS

It might seem somewhat odd to discuss treatment of behaviour problems close to the beginning of a chapter on intervention for SLDs. But, given the data offered earlier for the primacy of behaviour problems in both the early development, and the maintenance of SLDs, particularly for boys, there are powerful arguments for considering this issue early when thinking about the design of effective intervention. So this will be dealt with briefly as an important prelude to the consideration of remedial programmes for SLDs.

In recent years there has been a major growth in emphasis on early intervention for BPs, and indications that behavioural family intervention methods can bring about positive changes, thus reducing the likelihood of a poor behavioural and academic outcome for the at-risk child. These early intervention programmes emphasise improving parenting skills, as well as enriching the child's social and cognitive development and peer interaction skills (Sanders, 1995; Webster-Stratton & Herbert, 1994).

Training programmes for parents of young children to assist them to deal effectively with aggressive, disruptive, oppositional, and dysregulated behaviour can go a long way to reducing the risk for problems in both home and school settings. Such programmes usually include factors such as:

- increasing positive attention and rewards, when a child is behaving appropriately;
- developing effective discipline strategies such as clear and definite instructions which are not too frequently given, i.e. are concentrated on agreed "important" issues, rather than nagging about everything;
- using consequences such as removal of privileges, or removal from the scene of conflict when the child continues to create difficulties; and,
- use of inductive reasoning and communication which is attuned to the child's developmental level, to model ways of negotiation that will foster the ability to think and reason about problem solving.

The Triple P (Positive Parenting of Preschoolers) (Sanders, 1995) is one model of this kind of programme which is producing promising results in Australian pre-schoolers (see Sanders & Dadds, 1993, for a review).

Pre-school and school-based behavioural intervention programmes incorporating similar principles and involving parents and teachers as partners in finding better ways to manage children with adjustment problems are also highly recommended.

For socially disadvantaged families whose children may be at increased risk for the combination of BPs and SLDs, and who tend to be less readily engaged in behavioural intervention programmes, special efforts are needed to keep families involved and motivated, to deal with associated problems such as marital or lone parenting difficulties and lack of social support, and to build effective communication between school and home (e.g. Reid, 1993).

Long-term follow-up of families and children who have been involved in parenting and behaviour-management programmes is encouraging, with positive effects on academic progress, and on emotional and behavioural adjustment persisting though adolescence (Forehand & Long, 1988; Long, Forehand, Wierson, & Morgan, 1994; Sanders, 1995). But it must be conceded that older children and adolescents with entrenched learning and behaviour problems especially of the antisocial/delinquent type are notoriously hard to help, and their prognosis is poor. This emphasises the fact that early intervention is a very important and primary aspect of policies and practices in prevention or reduction of SLDs.

REVIEW OF INTERVENTIONS FOR SLD

It is best to be honest about the difficulties we have with finding successful interventions for specific learning difficulties. We still do not have sufficient research to be able to claim that early intervention will prevent or "cure" SLDs, although we have plenty of promising signs that it can make a substantial positive difference for many children (see e.g. review by Adams, 1990).

There is no clearly identified intervention or treatment currently or previously available which is entirely successful in overcoming the problems of children with established SLDs. We are quite skilled at assessment and in understanding the nature of the difficulties these children show. We have not been nearly so skilled in designing and evaluating effective treatment. There may be a variety of reasons for this.

The most obvious one is that every child is different, hence we need to find individually tailored programmes for each child which directly address his or her specific problems. Such approaches are extremely costly in time and resources and few educational facilities have access to the level of resources required for individualised, intensive programmes. But the common arrangement in schools with limited resources, of putting together a small group of children with a heterogeneous collection of problems, and giving them all a small amount of undifferentiated coaching in reading or maths is definitely not the most effective use of resources.

Another reason may be that most SLD children get too little, too late. The secondary consequences of SLD such as low motivation, dislike of school and academic pursuits, lack of self-esteem and self-confidence, with a history of being seen as a failure, can lead the child (or adolescent) to strong avoidance of anything to do with reading, writing, and maths. This can make intervention a very difficult undertaking with so much resistance and despair to overcome. It is also perhaps why some particular individual educators can achieve good results regardless of their methods, just because they are able to engage, inspire, and *motivate* SLD children through the warmth, and strength of their personal relationships with them. They are able to inspire hope!

Fashions change considerably in this field, so apart from the general paucity of research evaluating remedial methods, it is hard to build up a cumulative picture of effectiveness because of constant change. For example, a review of neuropsychologically based remedial reading procedures published in 1982 by Evans, covered multisensory approaches, perceptual motor training, movement therapies, inter-hemispheric integration, and biofeedback, and was hopeful about them all. A review published eight years later, (Scruggs & Wong, 1990) covered strategy deficit models, mnemonic instruction, content enhancement, social and behavioural interventions, and self-recording interventions. Although cautious, this review was also hopeful.

It is not surprising that professionals as well as parents become bewildered by the plethora of theories and treatments offered, especially when there are no guidelines or data to help them judge what works and what doesn't. Many enthusiastically advertised interventions appear to be based on neurological and neuropsychological theory, but so far these appear to be fruitless unless they also take into account the psycholinguistic processes inherent in the act of reading, or spelling, or the number skills inherent in maths.

Whatever the theoretical, philosophical, or practical orientation of the educational professional, *unless the deficient behaviour itself is addressed* (e.g. problems with actually recognising a word in print, or working out a multiplication problem), it is likely that efforts will be wasted. We still do not know a great deal about which brain processes directly link in to problems with learning of either general or particular kinds. Treatments based on speculative "neurological" theory, especially in the face of the enormous individual differences within a population of SLD children, are hard to justify, particularly if they neglect the specific skill training aspects.

TREATMENTS OF DOUBTFUL VALIDITY

Another hindrance to progress is that because of the lack of success in this challenging field, there has been plenty of opportunity for purveyors of all kinds of doubtful treatments to gain the attention and confidence of parents and teachers who are literally desperate to find help and will accept anything that promises a "cure". This can happen even if they are offered absolutely no evidence of any kind (other than "fast talking") that an intervention will work.

Huge amounts of money, time, and energy have been expended on non-valid methods, and oceans of false promises and failed hopes have impeded the development of well-researched and demonstrably effective techniques. However, in any field where a problem or condition is not well understood and is resistant to successful standard treatment, and where there is room for mystification using speculative theories, there will always be claims of magical "cure-alls" which vulnerable people will be keen to try, each time a new fad or fashion emerges.

In the 1960s and 70s, the fashion was for remedial approaches to reading using "visual perceptual training". This was very wasteful, because the visual perceptual activities offered were very distant from the kind of linguistic processing that is central to reading. Visual perceptual abilities do not play a major role in the critical early learning stages of word identification by comparison with language abilities (assuming of course that vision is adequate for "seeing" the letters). Thus, doing things with eyes is not likely to be particularly helpful. Evaluation of perceptual training methods has shown that these approaches are not effective in improving the reading skills of SLD children. But many years were lost until this fashion faded away.

Unfortunately unsubstantiated visual treatments of this kind often make a return to the fray. As noted in Chapter 5 "behavioural optometrists" have taken it upon themselves in recent years to diagnose and treat SLDs using visual "eye-skilling" training and perceptual exercises, in the absence of any evidence whatsoever that what they are doing has a rational theoretical basis, or any long-term beneficial effect on SLD children. A wide variety of non-language-related treatment programmes such as motor activities (trampolining, swinging, rolling, and balancing practice), drug treatment, eye movement training, wearing tinted lenses and filters, "teaching to the right hemisphere", kinesiology, and the like, cannot be supported as remedies for reading and spelling difficulties on scientific grounds. Their connections to reading and spelling are entirely obscure.

Unfortunately the proponents of these kinds of treatments do not provide us with any systematic descriptions or evidence for the effects of what they offer; their claims are most commonly based on clinical anecdotes.

The validity of remedial methods can only really be shown by scientific studies comparing treated and untreated children who are similar in all respects other than that one group is treated with the particular method, and the other is not. The reading progress of both groups of children over the short and the long term needs to be evaluated to see if it shows any effects of treatment. It is, of course, not acceptable to leave needy children untreated for the sake of science, but this can be attended to by treating the comparison group after the conclusion of the controlled intervention study.

However what frequently happens is that if a particular method receives substantial media exposure, it is followed by financial support from government or private sources, and attracts many adherents. A new fashion quickly takes off only to fade some years later as hopes are not fulfilled. As Gredler (1990) has noted, the cycle of acceptance and rejection of therapies in this field continues endlessly.

Behavioural methods to treat SLDs came to the fore in the 1970s and 80s, and although these were soundly based theoretically, in applying rewards for effort and for successful learning of new skills, they are simply not enough to deal with the serious cognitive and language-processing problems of most SLD children. More attention to the specifics of these processes is mandatory. Even some of the most enthusiastic proponents of vision-based treatments will concede that unless the basic building blocks of word knowledge are there, treatment based on notions of visual defects are unlikely to make any difference to the level of reading skill. The same principles apply to the use of behavioural methods.

REALISTIC EXPECTATIONS

We may also have to accept that there are some individuals who will never master one or more of the three Rs to a level that Western society finds satisfactory. For whatever reason, they may find it impossible to profit by the kinds of reading instruction we have to offer. We do not look down on people who cannot learn to play the piano, or hit a golf ball skilfully, despite good instruction; we should accept that problems with literacy or numeracy do not mean that an individual cannot make a worthwhile contribution to society and feel himself or herself a valuable person. Hence adaptation of educational and employment goals for some individuals may be necessary, with a focus on their strengths in other areas of functioning, and an emphasis on vocational objectives that are less dependent on literacy and numeracy skills.

This is an argument for greater community acceptance of, and respect for individual differences in levels and kinds of competencies.

EVALUATION RESEARCH

There is a shortage of studies evaluating the relative efficacy of different remedial teaching methods. Similarly, there are few data on the best way to go about teaching the skills of reading or mathematics to all children in the classroom. As noted earlier, this latter issue is not of predominant concern, because most children learn to read and to calculate no matter how they are taught. What is more troubling is that much *remedial* teaching reflects the philosophical persuasion of the particular teacher rather than having an empirical base. In practice, this means that LD children often receive only a "reheated" version of the common curriculum whether it is suited to their needs or not.

Code or phonological-based methods have been well supported in many remedial studies (e.g. Gittleman & Feingold, 1983), although they are rarely contrasted with other "top down" or language experience type interventions, and methodological rigour is often lacking in this research.

Comprehensive aggregated analyses of SLD interventions have also shown clearly that the closer the remedial method programme is to the deficit being treated (e.g. word analysis and synthesis for reading disability), the greater the chances of success. Most research supports the notion that because reading is a language-based, or psycholinguistic skill, then some kind of language-focused programme is going to be required for remediation. The best-documented efficacy is for phonetically based remedial programmes, although this does not mean that it is the best or the only treatment for every SLD child.

Lyon, Moats, and Flynn (1988) reported a study of treatment using a "synthetic phonics" approach which involves systematic instruction in saying the letter sounds in words, then blending them to decode new words. In this method, children are taught rules such as the correct sound of *a* in the words hat, sat, mat etc., or the sounds of letter combinations such as *sh*, *tr* etc. This is followed by repeated practice in sound blending, with exemplar words. Lyon et al. investigated whether different sub-groups of SLD children profited particularly well with this method according to how well it matched their neuropsychological profile of strengths and weaknesses. This is called a "diagnosis by treatment" study. After 30 hours of phonics instruction, comparisons were made of the different sub-types, in the amount of gains made in reading. The group with the *least* problems (a *normal* neuro-psychological profile) made the most gains, followed by those with visual–motor integration problems (for this latter group of children, phonic skills seemed to be already present as shown in their ability in reading regular words, so they had a good starting base). The other four sub-types in their study who were characterised by linguistic handicaps of varying types and severity (see Chapter 5), made minimal gains, and could not be said to have benefited from the phonics intervention.

This research suggests that the children who gained most were those with the least level of handicap in decoding skills, a finding that is repeated in many studies which are dominated by results showing the influence of initial severity on the outcome of remediation. Moreover, the children in this study were 11 to 12 years old, hence it is possible that for many of the more severely RD individuals, this was another example of too little, too late.

Early intervention with phonological awareness training is advocated by many reading researchers. Byrne and Fielding-Barnsley (1993) have developed a phonemic awareness programme for pre-schoolers which has shown promising results in follow-up into primary school. Children who mastered the contents of their programme were better readers and spellers in preparatory (kindergarten) grades. Beneficial effects on reading were still evident in a follow-up to Grade 2 (Byrne & Fielding- Barnsley, 1995). Like the much quoted work of Bradley and Bryant (1983), this supports the value of a phonological approach to training and enhancing reading and pre-reading skills in young children.

Other word-analysis-based methods such as teaching children to segment words into syllables, rather than phonemes; or to use orthographic rules (e.g., when two vowels are side by side as in e-a, the sound is that of the first letter), have also been shown to be helpful.

Lovett, Benson, and Olds (1990) have attempted to assess the variations in response to differing remedial approaches by sub-groups of RD children with differing patterns of deficits. A group of "accuracy-disabled" children (those who were stuck at the early stage of reading and could not reliably identify single words), was compared with a group of "rate-disabled" children (those who could recognise words but were slow in reading and poor in understanding of text). The former group made significant gains only when provided with phonologically based intervention, while the latter group made gains with both phonologically and whole-word-based intervention. These kinds of "aptitude by treatment" based evaluations may contribute to greater cost effectiveness in the long term, by comparison with omnibus or non-individualised approaches. Nevertheless, sub-types of SLD children are not simply differentiated on the basis of reading styles, but will vary according to the *stage* of reading acquisition that they are at, or the relative severity of disability, to use a plainer term. Type and severity of problems are difficult to disentangle, and make these kinds of studies a great challenge.

Lovett et al. (1990) found that pre-treatment deficits (i.e. severity) were the best predictors of response to their remedial interventions. The notion of a continuum of disability rather than sub-types of disabilities may be a more realistic way of viewing the difficulties of the majority of SLD children. It should not be surprising that children who are less handicapped to begin with are likely to be able to take advantage of remedial help more easily, and to do relatively better in the longer term.

At this stage of research into reading and spelling remediation, we have perhaps most to learn from well controlled research studies such as that reported by Hatcher, Hulme, and Ellis (1994). These authors were testing a "phonological linkage hypothesis" which suggests that "training in phonological skills in isolation from reading and spelling skills may be much less effective than training which forms explicit links between children's underlying phonological skills and their experiences in learning to read" (Hatcher et al., 1994, p.42). The RD children in their intervention programme, who were 7 years old, were divided into four groups, matched on age, IQ, and reading ability. Group 1 was given an integrated programme of phonological training combined with reading and writing of words and letters. Group 2 was given phonological training alone, while Group 3 was given the reading instruction only. That is, the latter two comparison groups had only one component while the first group had a combination of both. The fourth group, which received their usual classroom teaching without any special intervention, constituted a control or comparison group. All children were given the same tests of literacy-related skills before and after the training intervention and were followed up again nine months after the programme had ceased.

The children were also tested on arithmetic to assess whether any intervention might have "non-specific" effects on academic achievement. If arithmetic skills improved as much as reading skills, it would be less likely that the particular reading-based intervention was operating in a specific way to affect reading and spelling, rather than simply improving the children's general level of academic progress.

At the end of the remedial programmes, the phonological plus reading combination group did consistently better than the other two remediated groups on reading tests. In fact the single method groups did very little better than the control group. The same result was obtained with spelling measures. None of the treated groups showed any difference from the untreated group on the arithmetic measure. The "linkage" hypothesis was clearly supported, because only the children whose phonological training was linked to practice in reading and writing of words showed significant improvement.

The durability of the effects was also evident nine months later when the children given the integrated package were still well ahead of the other groups. However the improvements made by this group in spelling during the training period did not last, emphasising just how challenging it is to find a way to improve spelling with RD children.

Hatcher et al. (1994) also stressed that while the gains in reading were still significant at nine months follow-up, they did diminish. Such a finding reinforces yet again the fact that RD children need ongoing help; just plugging the gap at one point in time is not likely to be enough to overcome the difficulties they have.

This intervention study also assessed the particular contribution of the phonological training component in influencing reading gains. The group given only this training showed the best improvement on tests of phonological skills; however this was not matched by overall improvements in literacy skills. By contrast, although the group given the integrated programme did not make significant gains on tests of phonological skills, they were clearly able to derive benefit from the combination of approaches in achieving the most improved reading and spelling scores.

This study is important for several reasons. First, it supports the claim that phonological skills training must be integrated with actual word-reading practice to be maximally effective. Second, it suggests that phonological skills may be *necessary* for learning to read, but they may not be *sufficient*. Improvements in reading in RD children may not always come from phonological training alone. Third, phonological skill training did not improve spelling in this study, whereas those theories that stress the central role of phonology in spelling would have predicted that it would.

Fourth, the results are consistent with a number of other research findings with children of different ages, (Byrne & Fielding-Barnsley, 1995; Iversen & Tunmer, 1993; Lundberg, Frost, & Petersen, 1988) which show that an integrated package that includes phonological skills *within* meaning-based approaches such as Clay's (1985) Reading Recovery programme (see later) is more effective than purely reading instruction. Recent studies, including those reported by Lovett et al. (1994), and Wise and Olson (1995), have suggested that just teaching phonological processing skills might not be sufficient to produce major gains in *fluent* reading. This may need additional strategy training, skill consolidation, automatisation, and flexibility, so that reading for meaning can be enhanced.

By contrast with the abundant literature concerned with reading problems and remediation, there is little available regarding mathematics problems, their treatment, and their outcome. For remediation of mathematical difficulties, too little is known to allow reasonable conclusions concerning which methods work, for which kinds of MD children, at which level of competence, whether they have a single-area deficit or a combination with literacy problems. A review of research into mathematics instruction for SLD students by Mastropieri, Scruggs, and Shiah (1991) found that various forms of behavioural intervention including reinforcement, modelling, demonstration, and feedback were effective in increasing skill acquisition and fluency. Cognitive interventions such as goal setting, self-instruction and strategy training with verbalisation and feedback, and word problem solving strategies increased performance and independence in computation and problem solution. Other alternative interventions like cooperative classroom learning, computer assisted learning, videodiscs, and peer tutoring were also helpful. Skill-based teaching to clear objectives seemed to be the underlying factor in positive effects. Because the review said little about the specific characteristics of LD children in the evaluation studies, it is unclear to which population of MD children the results might apply. Evaluation of interventions for MD is an important but undeveloped research area.

PRINCIPLES OF INTERVENTION

Two underlying principles of intervention need to be considered. The first is that for almost every SLD child, individual one-to-one intervention will be the optimal procedure. Small group teaching, while more economical in teacher time, often does not allow the teacher to attend sufficiently to individual SLDs in an intensive way; hence any impact is diluted. As most SLD children's needs are substantial, any dilution will reduce the effectiveness of intervention.

The second principle is more controversial. Should one teach to strengths, i.e. building further on capacities the child has, such as good visual skills compared with poor auditory ones; or should one teach to weakness, i.e. try to plug the gaps where the child is deficient in particular capacities and processes? There is insufficient research to make generalised conclusions about this point, even though some writers argue strongly that greater gains are made by teaching through strengths.

A persuasive argument may be made, however, that for children with reading problems who have some strengths in whole word (visual), recognition but very poor phonological skills, it would be remiss not to "plug the gap" and teach these latter skills, because this gives them an additional strategy for decoding unknown words. There is no reason why this cannot be done in a context of also emphasising strengths with visual word memory where these are present.

That is, the optimum approach is likely to be phonics training for children who lack such strategies, but also including a visual over-view strategy applied to words and to sentences. Otherwise, the reader trained to depend on phonological strategies may not always make sense of the sound representations he or she constructs, and may lose the overall meaning of the passage as he or she engages in phonological translations. Such a reader will also be slow and laborious in reading, and will be handicapped when trying to read irregular words which cannot be accurately translated via phonological analysis.

With regard to the strength versus weakness debate, it is important to return to the argument that diagnosis and assessment should not be an end in itself, but should be "prescriptive", i.e. should lead to the development and recommendation of strategies and methods of individually based intervention, which are logical and reasonable given the particular difficulties and strengths identified. Specific plans for remediation should flow directly from the findings of the assessment, which should have pinpointed the particular problems for the child at both a functional (i.e. how the child actually goes about trying to read or spell), and a cognitive neuropsychological level (i.e. what are the underlying abilities such as verbal memory, for example, that are impaired and which may handicap the child in learning academic skills). Failure to move from assessment through to thoughtful and well-informed prescription may lead to ineffective and wasteful remedial time and effort, as "omnibus" treatments are applied to children whether they suit the particular disabilities or not.

Despite these recommendations, it has to be conceded that at the present state of knowledge we cannot say that this prescriptive approach has received sufficient research and practical attention to assess whether it will always provide the best answer to the challenge of treatment. Much more research is needed with larger samples of children, to assess SLD sub-type to treatment links, as well as the effects of individually profiled prescriptive programmes on the targeted SLDs (see Hooper & Willis, 1989, for summary of studies to date).

As SLDs are multi-dimensional problems it is rational to consider a multi-faceted approach to treatment. Certainly one particular intervention at one point in time is unlikely to produce lasting effects. It is also critical in many cases to complete a *behavioural assessment* as a large proportion of SLD children have problems with regulating and managing their own behaviour; they have poor attentional processes, high levels of impulsivity, and deficient behavioural control. If these are not tackled, the child may not be in the best condition to profit from remedial teaching no matter how well prescribed and presented. If a child is constantly fidgeting, getting up from his or her seat, tuning in on the activities of other children and interfering with their work, he or she is a poor candidate for special teacher attention in reading, spelling, or mathematics.

This chapter concludes with a brief summary of a comparative analysis of intervention effectiveness in SLD, published in 1990 by Scruggs and Wong.

One way to synthesise the results of many research studies looking at the same or similar phenomena is to conduct a meta-analysis. Such an analysis is based on the *size* of a change in score following treatment, or the *strength* of any effects shown (say, for example, average improvement in reading, spelling, or arithmetic scores in groups of SLD children) after an intervention has been used. This is done by surveying "effect sizes" across many studies, which makes it possible to suggest whether any intervention effects are truly meaningful or whether they have only a small and insignificant impact on outcome. Kavale (1988) reported a meta-analysis which showed that treatments such as perceptual motor training, diet (often used for children with Hyperactivity and Attention Deficits as well as SLD), "modality training" (teaching in accord with assessed modality preference patterns, such as auditory or visual), or placement in a special class, had no discernible positive effects on cognitive or academic achievement. By contrast, "psycholinguistic training" in verbal expression and verbal association (a top-down and language-focused approach to SLDs) did produce significant effect sizes or levels of improvement.

In this same study, the effects of treatment with stimulant medication (frequently prescribed for ADHD and learning problems), were also evaluated. Significant positive effects were shown for behavioural outcomes (such as improved compliance, attentional skills, social interaction skills, behavioural control in the classroom etc.) with lesser but still positive effects on cognitive functioning and reading and spelling performance. It is likely that the academic effects of medication are indirect ones, with the improved behavioural control assisting learning, rather than the medication itself being the operative factor in affecting academic skills. Additional analyses looking at early intervention and behaviour modification in the classroom also showed significant positive effects.

This apparently encouraging picture, however, must be tempered by the finding that there was tremendous individual variation in response to these different treatments. Thus Kavale (1988) suggested that interventions are characterised more by variability than generalised benefit in their effects. This makes it difficult to predict for any individual whether an intervention will be effective.

SUMMARY

Generalised claims about intervention benefits need to be cautious, although it is safe to say:

a) Direct individualised teaching which is focused on deficits and strengths identified from thorough testing will be important.
b) Sequence and structure in the programme as well as eliciting high levels of student motivation are essential.
c) Integrated packages such as the one described for reading remediation in the Hatcher et al. (1994) study have strong support.
d) Focusing only on weaknesses or strengths may limit efficacy; treatment should attend to both assets and deficits.
e) Long term monitoring and follow up will be needed.

In general it is a truism to say that early identification and treatment is optimal, so the earlier LD children are assessed and provided with help, the better. But we should not give up on older children with LDs presenting for help quite late in development. There are many clinical anecdotes of teenagers and adults who decide to overcome their reading problems after they had left school. With strong motivation and effort, they succeeded in becoming at least functional, if not expert, readers. Moreover, there are always those who persist in working on their problems, who succeed in going on to post-secondary school education , and who achieve their career goals despite their difficulties, even if expenditure of heroic effort is required.

CHAPTER EIGHT

Remedial techniques and resources

Approaches to teaching reading in the classroom, and to helping children who have reading and spelling difficulties are sometimes dichotomized into two basic methods. One emphasises reading for meaning and concentrates on whole word methods, or language experience. This is sometimes called a "top-down" principle. The other emphasises a "code" approach and involves phoneme awareness training, direct phonics teaching, and methods that include analysis of syllables and intra-word units. This has been called the "bottom-up" approach. The methods detailed here usually fall into one of these categories, although as was argued in the preceding chapter, a total remedial focus on one or the other will not be adequate to produce fluent reading in the SLD child. The theoretical position that emerges from the material in previous chapters is clearly one that supports the essential nature of phonological skills in reading and spelling, albeit within a context of integrating the sub-skills to facilitate text comprehension.

There are countless books for parents and professionals on the market which profess to assist with reading and mathematics problems. Although many of them are reasonably well supported theoretically, i.e.

they are based on psycholinguistic and cognitive theory which is well accepted, few of the programmes and methods they propose have actually been evaluated to determine their success in remediation. Hence their credibility is undermined by the fact that writers rarely produce empirical evidence of the effectiveness of their interventions. Case histories and anecdotes are often used to support favoured methods but they do not constitute acceptable objective evidence of the worth of a programme. Bearing in mind the arguments for careful assessment and targeted prescription for intervention in SLDs maintained throughout this book, finding the right method in the right book for your SLD child would be very much a hit and miss approach. Nevertheless those books that are acceptable theoretically, and which can demonstrate some research-based evaluations can be very useful and enlightening for professional and parent readers.

And parents and teachers find it helpful to have an instructional guide or framework to follow when they are trying to help the SLD child.

An example of a book that grew out of theory and research and which does have published research support, is Bradley's (1980) *Assessing reading difficulties* which emphasises a code-based or phonological intervention. Another useful booklet is that by Glynn, McNaughton, Robinson, and Quinn (1979) called *Remedial reading at home: Helping you to help your child*, (see later under parent tutoring). Research studies support the value of their approach, both in the classroom and with home tutoring.

Most of these kinds of books are written by people who are extremely concerned about the general lack of success in treating SLD children, and who believe that their preferred method will help. Indeed, many of them have worked with SLD children and found that they have been able to make a difference. However, in most cases it is impossible to know whether progress is the result of the method, the characteristics of the child, the specific SLD characteristics treated, the skills and dedication of the teacher, the support received at home, or some other factor(s). Nor is it possible in most cases to know whether any progress is maintained once the programme has ceased.

This view is the hard-nosed "scientific" one which stresses the need for proper evaluation of a treatment. All children deserve such care in making decisions about their learning needs, just as is required in decisions about other aspects of their health and welfare. However it should also be admitted that there is plenty of evidence that teacher characteristics such as warmth and concern for the child, and the ability to inspire confidence and to elicit attention and motivation, are powerful ingredients in any intervention. These factors have been resistant to measurement and evaluation, but their influence is powerful.

PROGRAMMED LEARNING

There are some programmed learning systems that go beyond the books about "how to remediate" referred to earlier. The DISTAR (Direct Instructional System for Teaching Reading and Arithmetic) method is one that has been used for teaching LD children in primary school grades.

One DISTAR example provided by Engelmann and his colleagues (Engelmann & Bruner, 1969) is a systematic "morphographic spelling" programme which is based on the fact that words and their parts can be analysed as morphographs or meaningful sub-components of words (within the word "content", "con" is a morphograph and so is "tent"). Systematic learning of morphographs, it is believed, will help children to analyse words into meaningful parts before they try to spell them. It is a way of making a new or difficult word easier to attempt. This programme, which provides workbooks for child, and for parent or teacher, begins by assessing the current skill level of the SLD child, and then moves through graded lessons from very simple to very complex. Continuous monitoring of progress is maintained with tests given regularly and frequently. The programme can also be used with groups of children, providing of course that their needs are similar.

The DISTAR reading programme, by the same authors, is based on similar learning principles and uses a "synthetic phonics approach". In this approach, specific grapheme–phoneme relationships are directly taught, and then followed up with training in blending sounds. However, additional work to achieve fluency with reading will be necessary as this DISTAR programme is somewhat laborious and emphasises decoding skills, perhaps at the expense of reading for meaning.

Programmed instruction systems such as the DISTAR models can be very helpful especially for the highly motivated and intelligent SLD child. But as with all approaches, they require a high level of dedication on the part of the tutor (who may be a parent or other helper as well as a teacher), and the child, to persevere. The educational and psychological principles upon which these kinds of programmes are based are excellent, but there is little research literature to underpin claims for their effectiveness.

THE GILLINGHAM AND STILLMAN APPROACH

The Remedial Training for Children with Specific Disabilities in Reading, and Penmanship (Gillingham & Stillman, 1979), is a development of the phonologically based Orton-Gillingham programme for RD children which at the time of its first promulgation in the 1930s reflected Orton's theory of reading. It has proved very influential and enduring, and has been reprinted many times. The main characteristics of the Gillingham and Stillman (1979) programme are: a rule-based approach; teaching phonics directly, with the introduction of letter names and sounds followed by blending skills; the use of a multi-sensory technique involving teaching through visual, auditory, and kinaesthetic modalities (naming letters, sounding letters, tracing letters with fingers); and a step by step approach from simple to complex.

Core features of the method include the building of grapheme–phoneme associations; blending of phonemic segments, syllables, and use of pseudowords to instil principles (pseudowords are nonsense words such as "mip" which give the child practice in using sounding-out skills); generating rules, and fixing them in memory through kinaesthetic reinforcement using tracing and/or writing, i.e. seeing, hearing, saying, tracing, and writing. Overall this programme provides a synthesis of primarily "bottom-up" and rule-based approaches.

There are reports of success with this approach but very few controlled research studies with carefully defined groups of SLD children, and it is hard to find comparisons with other methods (see Ansara, 1982). A study by Kline and Kline, (1975) reported gains for children of all ages including adolescents, with the Orton-Gillingham approach. Hornsby and Miles (1980) also claim improvement in reading and spelling in more than 80% of severely RD children with this approach.

These methods have been very influential for many years in remedial reading territory, and many practitioners have been trained in them and are confident in supporting their use. Phonological emphases may be more successful because they apply well to both reading and spelling pathways; using only whole word (top-down) methods, leaves out a major remedial approach to word analysis and word production.

Another advocate of multi-sensory teaching is Hulme (1981), who claims that many SLD children have verbal memory problems that hinder their learning of reading, which in the beginning stages at least requires the active memorisation of a word and its written form. Hulme advocated the use of letter tracing as a useful way to incorporate an additional sensory input (touch) into the learning to read process. This adds in visual and kinaesthetic clues to the process. That is, the child sees, says, writes, and feels the word. In this way, it can be argued, all the senses are involved and those that are strong can compensate for those that are weak. As with so many approaches this is very appealing intuitively, but once again there are minimal empirical data to support the claims for its usefulness as a remedial method.

COMPUTER ASSISTED LEARNING

With the rapid proliferation of computer assisted methods of all kinds of learning and communication, the potential for Computer Assisted Learning (CAL) to help SLD children seems immense. CAL has a number of strengths including: the computer can be programmed to respond and adapt to the pace and progress of the individual student; it can provide immediate feedback about whether responses are correct or not, in a non-threatening objective way; it allows the student to use immediate feedback to change responses, because it provides an instant two-way information loop process; it can be especially appealing to children who find computers interesting, non-threatening, and controllable in ways in which classroom instruction cannot always be; it can be adapted to provide instruction in whichever area is most needed for the individual student (Cumming, Galante, & Prior, 1987).

Despite these theoretical advantages, at this stage of CAL development there is not a great deal of systematic and objective documentation of short- or long-term effectiveness. Nor are there data concerning the advantages of CAL over other methods. It may be that the interpersonal approach supplied by a warm and sympathetic teacher is central to effective teaching, hence CAL by itself will always have its limitations.

Gredler (1992) reports on a 1983 study by McDermott and Watkins which showed no clear advantage of CAL over traditional methods of remediation and which suggested that a combination of methods will be needed depending on the nature and severity of the individual LD. Olson and Wise (1992) have compared various methods of teaching reading using CAL, by varying the type and amount of phonological versus whole word based remediation within the CAL programme. They found that CAL was more effective than a standard remedial reading method, and its effects were moderated by the initial levels of phonological abilities in their groups. Type of instruction interacted with severity of RD in the outcome of the training, and the best predictor of gain scores was initial level of phonological awareness. Olson and Wise noted the enthusiasm and confidence generated by CAL in teachers, parents, and children. Their work adds to that supporting the value of phonologically based remedial instruction, as well as the powerful effects of enhancing motivation in SLD children.

Olson and Wise also emphasise that individual instruction increases programme effectiveness and that CAL cannot be expected to take over from teachers in helping RD children. CAL appears to be a useful supplementary technique which, when combined with individualised teaching, will produce greater gains than individualised instruction alone.

Spelling remediation using CAL also shows considerable promise, (see e.g. Fawcett, Nicholson, & Morris, 1993), and researchers such as those cited here have been concerned with evaluating differing types of presentation of material, varying techniques, and the influence of stage of learning. For example, different approaches may be required depending on whether the child is at the alphabetic or the orthographic (see Chapter 2) stage of reading and spelling.

O'Hare et al. (1991) note the existence of computer software for helping with maths problems, although they do not provide any data on their efficacy.

CAL is still a developing tool for remedial instruction; it has great promise as a contributor to effective means of helping SLD children, and the next few years will probably bring further programme development and evaluation of its value.

The *Journal of Computer Assisted Learning* is a good source of research papers on this topic for those considering this kind of approach to remediation.

READING RECOVERY

Based on the work of the eminent New Zealand educationalist Marie Clay (1985), a programme called "Reading Recovery" has been widely adopted over the past decade. It is a prime example of a meaning emphasis, whole-word or language-experience approach to reading (although it does not totally neglect phonological skills). The whole language learning approach is a philosophy rather than a specified method for teaching reading, hence it is very difficult to define and to compare with other approaches such as the phonics one which is more systematically detailed in its methods.

Children showing delays in reading in the second year of primary school (Grade 1), and who are considered "at risk" for school failure are selected for the Reading Recovery programme. Children are withdrawn from class for remedial sessions. As soon as the children have met criteria for improvement (or come to the end of the school year) they resume the usual curriculum. This programme is not so much provided for diagnosed SLD children, but is designed for those who might be considered at risk after poor progress in the first year of instruction. Teachers are given special training in implementing this system which is based on individualised one-to-one or small group sessions. Parents as well as teachers are encouraged to be involved in helping the children.

Results of the relatively few published evaluation studies from the USA, New Zealand, and Australia, are rather mixed, with some children becoming "normal" readers and others making little progress. Longer-term benefits are small although some adherents claim that the programme reduces the necessity to keep back children who are failing in Grade 1.

Because it primarily targets children who are too young at the Grade 1 stage to meet criteria for SLD, it is difficult to assess its value for LD children. Many children going through the programme would not be at risk for SLD but are perhaps "late maturers' who would progress normally in time, without intervention. A number of them may be cognitively handicapped to some unknown extent, and hence at risk because of such impairments rather than having specific LDs. Much of the evaluation research has been carried out by educators who, although demonstrating some gains for some children and good acceptance of the method, have not provided well-controlled studies of clearly defined groups of at-risk children followed over the longer term. Because this programme has rarely been compared with others, it is uncertain whether any gains are related to the nature of the particular programme or to the provision of individualised instruction which might be helpful no matter what its content was.

An evaluation study in New Zealand reported by Iversen and Tunmer (1993), in which a group receiving standard Reading Recovery tuition was compared with a group receiving an equivalent amount of the same tuition but with explicit phonological code instruction added, showed that the latter group made much quicker gains in reading skill. Furthermore, progress in Reading Recovery was strongly related to the initial level of phonological skills, a finding which echoes that of the CAL study described earlier.

Center, Wheldall, and Freeman (1992) have critically reviewed evaluation studies of Reading Recovery. They too stress the problems with many educational innovations, of which Reading Recovery is just one example. Such innovations begin with great enthusiasm, are widely disseminated despite the fact that they are not subject to scientific evaluation, but often descend into disappointment and eventual demise. Reviews of code (or bottom-up) emphasis, versus meaning (top-down) emphasis methods suggest advantages for the former over the latter. Moreover, the limited empirical data that do exist suggest that whole word approaches without the addition of phonics instruction are not adequate for RD children. Hence from a theoretical as well as a practical point of view the appropriateness of Reading Recovery for RD children has yet to be clearly demonstrated.

"TALKING" BOOKS

Talking book or "multiple oral re-reading" methods have been used with both adults and children (see Moyer, 1979), and can be helpful for developing fluency and confidence in reading text. In this method, the student (or the teacher) selects a preferred text or story, the teacher provides an audiotape of the story, the student listens and reads along with the tape while following the print in the text, as many times as is necessary to achieve fluency with that passage. The student next practises reading the text without the tape model, then is assessed on the passage by the teacher, who decides when there is sufficient fluency and accuracy to have the student move on to another story.

This procedure can be repeated (for as long as the student and teacher have motivation and patience), until a level of literacy is achieved that is satisfying to both parties. Passages of gradually increasing length and complexity are introduced as fluency grows. Individual preference combined with individual literacy needs would guide the choice of this as a preferred method, as there are no controlled evaluations of its efficacy by comparison with other methods. Its underlying principle is repeated practice until a certain level of mastery is reached. This can be particularly helpful for students who have achieved a reasonable level of single word recognition but who need help in increasing their rate and fluency so that they can process and remember the meaning of a story in a more effortless way.

PARENTS AS TUTORS FOR THEIR SLD CHILDREN

In recent years many schools have adopted policies and practices that encourage parents to become more actively involved in their children's learning. Such involvement can take many forms: from just reading to the child regularly, to hearing the child go through set homework each night, to actually participating in the classroom by acting as a tutor for children learning to read, and/or for those children who are struggling and need extra assistance which the teacher has no time to provide.

In some cases parents (or volunteer non-parents) come to the school regularly to provide help in the classroom.

In Britain, the "Haringey Reading Project" which involved parents in their (6–8-year-old) children's reading using paired reading methods, showed very positive effects up to at least three years after the project had ended (Hewison, 1988).

Glynn and his colleagues in New Zealand (see e.g. Glynn, Fairweather, & Donald, 1992) have developed a set of behaviourally based tutoring methods called "Pause, Prompt and Praise" which are designed for parents (or other tutors) to help children who are making slow progress with reading. The helper pauses when the child makes an error, to wait for him or her to self-correct. If this does not happen the helper offers various prompts such as a clue to meaning, or letter or sound cues, and then specifically praises the child's self-correction or response to the prompts. The integrity of this approach will be dependent on judicious choice of reading materials that are at an appropriate difficulty level. For example, if it is too hard there will be so many errors that the child cannot pick up the sense of the story. If it is too easy they have too little opportunity to try strategies and respond to prompts to learn more effective problem-solving. Glynn et al.'s small booklet called *Remedial reading at home: Helping you to help your child* (1979), is very useful for parents wanting to help their SLD child and needing some advice on a comfortable and helpful way to go about it.

Some parents who try to help their children with reading and mathematics can become impatient, frustrated, disappointed, and angry when they feel that their efforts are not leading to any changes, and that the child does not remember from one session to the next, the words he or she had learned to read or spell. This can lead to very negative parent–child dynamics, and deteriorating family relationships. Such a consequence should be avoided at all costs. Not every parent makes a good tutor, and some children will strenuously resist parents watching them struggle, and telling them what to do with reading. This is a sensitive area which needs thoughtful and considered decisions before setting up parent tutoring at home.

To carry out this treatment effectively, parents and teachers also need to develop a partnership so that they can work together. They need to agree on what the child needs to be reading, or which aspects of mathematics need special attention, and to monitor their own and the child's behaviour to make sure that progress is occurring and there are no negative psychological consequences.

PEER TUTORING

There have been a number of studies which have demonstrated that peers (usually somewhat older children) can be effective tutors for SLD children. The most common finding is that the tutoring benefits the tut*ors* just as much as the tut*ees*. It is likely that coaching in specific teaching strategies for tutors to use, such as the "paired reading" technique of Morgan and Ryan (1979), or the "Pause, Prompt, Praise" methods noted earlier, will provide greater gains than simply "reading together time", although this too can be helpful. Modelling, feedback, praise, and reinforcement used in the best traditions of behaviour therapy, are core methods. Enhancement of motivation through the SLD child's own self-selection of reading material, together with the positive social interactions with peers, can combine in a very effective approach especially when it is systematically and carefully managed. That is, it is not enough to just put children together to read, there needs to be programmed instruction, professional guidance, and consistent monitoring of the progress of tutors and tutees. Books used must be at the level of the tutee.

Limbrick, McNaughton, and Cameron (1985) claim substantial gains in reading selected books, for tutees and for tutors and propose a number of reasons for such improvements. For the tutee these include increased instructional time and the undivided attention of a peer, in a private and supportive situation; support and praise along with increasing independence; and the enhancement of fluency and comprehension through the use of questions and feedback. For the tutors, there are extra opportunities for reading at a level well within capacity; feelings of competence, responsibility, and self-esteem coming from being "the teacher"; and of course teaching something is an excellent way to learn it. Limbrick et al. suggest that there should be careful but short and simple training of tutors, frequent but short bursts of such reading interactions over a relatively brief period, of four to six weeks, and that evaluation of both tutor and tutee should be built in. They also suggest that the same peer-tutoring approaches can work for children struggling with maths.

COGNITIVE BEHAVIOURAL INTERVENTIONS

These kinds of interventions for SLD children rely on the teaching of "self-instruction". Using this approach, children are taught to talk themselves through problems to be solved, as an antidote to rushing impulsively and haphazardly into a task. This mode of intervention has broad applicability across all types of SLDs.

First a model demonstrates how to self-instruct by modelling the task approach, in speaking out loud to oneself, for example: *what kind of problem do I have here? ... what must I notice? ... what do I need to remember here? ... now where do I start, ... ah here by looking at the sign,* etc. The child then imitates this model as he or she approaches a task.

Gradually the learner moves through stages of less and less *overt* self-instruction until he or she is able to tackle problems with silent self-talk. Proponents of these methods stress the fact that academic failure can often be the result of the deficits in organised, planful, strategic behaviour which regulate the way a child goes about a task. SLD children also sometimes appear to lack the language skills that other children use to talk themselves through problems; that is, so-called "verbal mediation" processes or "task relevant private speech". They often need prompts from other people rather than generating them spontaneously. In addition they have often developed a sense of helplessness, lost their enthusiasm for tackling learning tasks, and have low productivity. Because of such multiple and complexly interwoven psychological and learning problems, using cognitive behavioural approaches makes good sense. Wong, Harris, and Graham (1991) have provided a review of studies of cognitive behavioural approaches for LD children and report positive results for reading comprehension, writing instruction, spelling, revising of work, and mathematical skills. Although strategy training and self-instruction techniques especially for children with impulsive and poorly organised approaches to learning are helpful, they are no panacea. The SLD child will still require teaching of word-analysis skills, or arithmetic operations, as well as task approach strategies. Many SLD children have difficulties with generalising learned strategies. They may apply strategies as specifically taught in one situation, but not produce them the next time a similar problem comes up. So generalisation strategies must also be taught, with many examples of when and how to apply previously learned solutions.

Metacognitive strategies, which are not dissimilar to the cognitive behavioural approach noted earlier, are believed to have considerable promise as generalisable techniques for SLD children. The aim of the metacognitive approach is to teach a repertoire of useful strategies which can be applied across a broad range of learning situations. At the same time, there should be provision of incentives and aids for the child to produce and to use appropriate strategies. Feedback and rewards will increase the chances of the strategies being applied across a range of learning tasks. Again, this approach is theoretically sound, and practically useful, but may have limited success especially when the child lacks the basic knowledge of what to apply to a problem, e.g. a sounding-out attack on a new word, or a way of remembering particular spellings, or the steps in a multiplication task.

REMEDIATING MATHEMATICAL DIFFICULTIES

Because so many children have a combination of literacy and numeracy problems, it is often difficult to know whether to focus on literacy and ignore or delay intervention in maths, or whether all areas should be included in a total programme. This decision will rest on thorough assessment of the child's needs, and his or her capacities for profiting from remedial instruction. It may be that the task of improving reading will be given priority and that maths will be attended to as a secondary line of assistance. Where maths is the major obstacle and literacy is less affected, the focus will be on the former.

Designing a remedial maths programme should follow on from clear identification of just what processes are deficient in the SMD child and what level of instruction is warranted. Programmed learning approaches such as the Science Research Associates (SRA) Arithmetic programme operate on this principle by assessing the child's current stage of competence and then beginning from there with graded teaching steps (as for reading and spelling noted earlier in the section on DISTAR).

Remedial approaches need to be clear about the necessary principles of programme design. These include: clarifying concepts by demonstrating them to the child in a number of different and interesting ways which are as *concrete* as possible and attuned to the child's level of interest and understanding; using a variety of aids such as familiar objects, or blocks or abacuses, which illustrate principles such as ordination, length, seriation etc.; and learning of rote counting sequences such as tables, counting backwards, counting by fives, tens, and so on.

Teaching sequential processes or steps so that they are reliably understood; providing verbal rules and routines; repetition and practice of each step before moving on to the next, are all essential principles of instruction.

Sufficient practice with highly motivating activities is absolutely essential, no matter what is being taught. The use of calculators can be encouraged once the operations to be performed are thoroughly understood.

Strang and Rourke (1985), in discussing remediation strategies, suggest concentration on verbal rather than visual approaches for SMD children; that is, to work through their strengths. Use of systematic, concrete, step by step verbal instructions, and getting the child to repeat aloud and then write the "recipe" is recommended. The child should be helped to record and then task-analyse his or her errors. The use of everyday living examples is important. Providing easily visible charts of number facts, e.g. tables and key reminders, can help. This "cookbook" approach, however, presupposes that the child can recognise the nature of the problem in order to know which recipe to use. Using assessment tools such as KeyMath, as was described in Chapter 3, can help to focus remedial programmes on specific areas of weakness for the individual child.

Most approaches recommend a sequence involving problem analysis, followed by concrete examples, moving to abstract principles and then applications to real-life problems. Recommendations for remediating mathematics are seriously limited by the dearth of published evaluation studies. However studies such as those reported by Rourke and Tsatsanis (1995) which use neuropsychological sub-typing analyses to connect deficits to remedial strategies in a strategic way, offer promise for future effective interventions.

REMEDIAL METHODS FOR SPELLING

In his book *Spel...is a four-letter word*, Gentry (1987) suggests a number of effective teaching strategies for children with difficulties in this area. These include frequent purposeful writing practice with labels, signs, plans, lists, recipes, letters, as well as stories; encouragement of "invented" spelling for new words at least in the early stages, to get children thinking about how words are constructed; de-emphasising correctness so that word study is a fun learning experience; self-correction of spelling to aid visual memory for words; and being aware of individual differences in instructional needs. Gentry also supports multi-sensory approaches using looking, saying, and writing of letters and words, in preference to simply repetitively re-writing words for which the correct spelling is given.

A recommended multi-sensory learning technique that focuses on spelling but also helps greatly with reading is the "Simultaneous Oral Spelling" (SOS) approach. This is a modified version of the procedures advocated by Gillingham and Stillman noted earlier. Bradley (1981) has proposed this modification as follows:

Children are taught to spell and read words using *sight, sound*, and *motor* repetition. They themselves choose the words they wish to learn, and no matter how unusual or eccentric their choice might be, this is an important motivating element which must remain the child's prerogative.

The following steps are followed with each word, with regular daily practice:

1.   The child suggests the word he or she wants to learn.
2.   The word is printed for him or her (or constructed with plastic letters).
3.   The child names the word.
4.   The child then writes the word, saying the alphabetic name of each letter as it is written.
5.   The child names the word again, and then checks against the model which remains on view, to see that he or she has written the word correctly.

Steps 2 through 5 are repeated twice more, with the model spelling covered when the child feels he or she can manage without it.

6.   The word is practised this way for several consecutive days until the child can reliably produce the correct spelling and reading.

New words can be introduced at every session, depending on the rate of progress, and the child's age and capacity to maintain concentration and effort. In this way a repertoire of known spellings is built up with good retention expected, especially with the multi-sensory approach. Bradley (1982) has demonstrated the effectiveness of this method, and highlighted the fact that all kinds of RD children with a variety of combinations of difficulties can learn to discriminate, to label, to analyse, organise, and remember, through the combined input of all modalities as they read, speak, and write. Prior et al. (1987) used this method with groups of children who varied in their pre-treatment ability to use phonological strategies in their reading. Their findings were essentially consistent with those reported for other methods of remediating reading and spelling reported in this chapter. The less handicapped the child, the greater the gains made; that is, severity of disability was the critical influential factor. In general, the children who were weakest on phonological skills benefited least from the SOS training, because this weakness was linked to severity of reading and spelling difficulties.

SUMMARY

This chapter has briefly described a range of remedial approaches for reading and spelling difficulties including Programmed Learning, phonologically based and multi-sensory methods such as that of Gillingham and Stillman, computer assisted learning, the Reading Recovery programme of Marie Clay, parent and peer tutoring systems, and cognitive behavioural interventions. Specific programmes designed for maths difficulties are not easy to find, although there are some good general principles available.

The last two chapters have provided a mixture of hope and concern. Hope because many children do improve if they are given enough of the kind of help that suits their problems; and concern because we cannot confidently assert that we have solved the difficulties of treating SLDs. Avoidance of unsubstantiated treatments whose promises are based on often nonsensical distortions of neurological theory is strongly recommended. Treatments whose methods are close in content to the deficit being treated, such as word-analysis strategies for reading and spelling problems, are generally much more effective than those that treat some cognitive function which is more distant from the actual deficit.

An important and recurring theme is the need to maintain the motivation and confidence of the SLD child so that he or she is willing to persist; and to stress the development of other areas of individual strength or competence which enhance self-esteem. Children need to be reassured that there are many areas of life, outside the classroom, that are important and fulfilling and in which they can have mastery experiences.

CHAPTER NINE

Recapitulation

What are the major messages of this book?

1. The definitional problems that have always plagued the SLD field are still in evidence, although they have not prevented a great deal of excellent research which has, at the very least, advanced our understanding of literacy problems. Debate will no doubt continue about how best to measure literacy and numeracy skills; about cut-off points, or discrepancy scores on various measures which attract specific diagnostic labels; and about how "pure" a syndrome, or a collection of signs and symptoms, must be to warrant a name like "specific learning difficulties'.

With regard to reading problems, we may reasonably question the use of diagnostic labels like dyslexia, IQ discrepant reading levels, specific reading retardation, backward reader, and the like, as there is no evidence to confirm the validity of such categories by any conventional criteria for the goodness of a diagnostic classification. Such criteria include: carefully defined sets of non-overlapping symptoms, response to treatment, course of the disorder, distinct aetiology, or long-term outcome. None of these criteria can be satisfactorily met in currently popular definitions of RD. Nevertheless at a clinical and educational level, we can agree quite well about which individuals have serious reading and spelling problems despite their normal overall intellectual ability, and that we need to do something about it.

There seems no good reason why "Developmental Reading Disorder" should be included in a *psychiatric* classification system such as the Diagnostic and Statistical Manual of the American Psychiatric Association (DSM-IV), or the World Health Organisation's International Classification of Diseases (ICD-10). Reading disability is neither a disease nor a psychiatric disorder, and there is a reasonable case for considering it the lower part of a continuum of reading capacity with no established pathological implications (Prior, 1989).

2. The causes of SLDs remain unknown, even though for a proportion of cases there will be evidence for organic involvement. However these children do not differ in the nature of their SLDs from idiopathic cases (those with no known cause). There are a number of neurologically oriented theories suggesting the possibility of brain dysfunction, especially involving the left hemisphere of the brain, but there is little evidence to endorse these theories despite many years of searching. For reading and spelling difficulties, there is evidence for genetic influence which helps us to understand why some affected children have difficulties. Current research suggests that the inherited "disability" may be facility with phonological decoding. There are likely to be a number of causes relevant in the development of SLDs; careful history taking and assessment may illuminate individual factors that are influential.

For problems with mathematics, too little is known to conclude that there are genetic factors, or indeed any other specific causes. We must await more research on this question especially in regard to children with *specific* problems with mathematics. The most rational conclusion based on current knowledge is that there are probably many causes of SMD also.

3. Prediction of who will develop LDs is not infallible, but we have some very good pointers or risk factors. These include behavioural problems especially of the attention deficit hyperactivity type; and, developmental language problems, most notably when the latter involve delays or deficits in phonemic awareness. Neither of these conditions is either necessary or sufficient for the development of LDs, and predicting which children are at risk remains a challenge. Less than perfect prediction, however, should not be seen as a discouragement to early intervention. It may be that we will have to put up with mistakes such as treating "false positives" (children suspected of SLDs but in whom they do not actually develop), and failure to identify children who really need help ("false negatives"), in order to catch a significant proportion of children who could be helped in the early stages, and for whom

successful early intervention can transform their educational experiences into successful ones.

4. For children with SLDs, the difficulties appear to be persistent for the majority of cases. But outcome could almost certainly be improved if better account was taken of the large quantity of knowledge that we have acquired about SLDs, and which we could apply to intervention more profitably, especially in the case of reading problems. The continual refrain concerning the need for more resources to be more readily available to apply to both early intervention or prevention, and to remedial teaching, requires more forceful advocacy. On the positive side, follow-up studies such as those of Maughan (1995) and others, show that SLD children often achieve reasonable levels of skill, can go on to further education and training, and find success and pride in employment.

5. Relatively little is known about numeracy problems, their cognitive underpinnings, their importance for long-term adjustment, and what to do about treating them. We know that maths problems co-occur with literacy problems in many cases, but that there are also a substantial proportion of the school population who do have specific difficulties with maths. We also know that individual profiles of maths difficulties differ; for example, a child may have some basic concepts but be very handicapped in operational mathematics or basic computational skills, or may have particular difficulty in applying what he or she knows in everyday life. It is not uncommon to find unevenness across the many different areas of mathematical knowledge. It has been repeatedly suggested in this book that this is an area greatly in need of more fine-grained research.

6. The relationships between SLDs and behaviour problems are firmly established and should be given more emphasis in designing interventions. This is especially the case for boys, who are at high risk for the combination of difficulties from an early age. Having both SLDs and behaviour problems is a particularly perilous combination for long-term outcome, with the likelihood of disadvantage piled on disadvantage, and persisting difficulties in employment and psychosocial functioning. Assessment and treatment of behavioural difficulties is as essential as attention to the learning problems, and as critical for improving prognosis.

7. SLDs in girls may be neglected because girls so rarely show externalising or disruptive behaviour problems which attract negative

attention to themselves. Hence they may be less likely than boys to attract any of the limited resources available for assistance; resources that are directed predominantly to children referred for clinical services. Recent community (non-clinical) studies finding almost as many girls as boys with reading and spelling problems reinforce the need to pay more careful attention to girls who are quietly struggling in the classroom.

8. Research into the evaluation of remedial methods in all areas of SLD has been in short supply, although the current level of research activity is encouraging, and better controlled and well-informed methods and evaluations may be increasing. Matching treatment to individual profiles of difficulties has always been part of the rhetoric of this area, but this precept has been slow to achieve widespread adoption and to produce profitable insights into the best way to go about helping LD children. It appears likely that individualised remedial instruction will always be required even though it is expensive. But home tutoring, peer tutoring, computer assisted instruction, cognitive strategy training, and systematic approaches centred around phonological and word-analysis skills can certainly help many SLD children.

Most current theory is strongly in support of the importance of phonological skills in learning to read, and emphasises the fact that a majority of RD children have problems in this area early in development and persisting through the school years. This knowledge should be helpful in guiding better-targeted remedial approaches in which teaching phonological strategies is critical to improvement in literacy skills.

9. Early intervention for children at risk of SLDs should be high priority for educationalists, and health professionals, bearing in mind that even a few children saved from a pathway to LDs and the accompanying distress, represents substantial profit. Pre-school-level intervention for children showing behavioural difficulties, and/or limited language competence, and especially poor self-regulation and attentional skills, has the potential to save a great deal of individual and community distress in the longer term. There is considerable intervention and follow-up work focused on early behavioural management and social learning skills being evaluated currently in a number of countries, which may lead to greater understanding of what works for which children (and families) over the long term.

10. Expert cognitive, language, educational, and neuropsychological assessment is mandatory in understanding the individual child and his

or her SLDs and in focusing intervention in optimal ways. Considerable expertise in assessment exists amongst health and educational professionals, but we need to translate assessment findings into effective assistance for the SLD child. Understanding what has gone wrong is important, but without follow-up resources to do something about the problems, it is of limited usefulness. Parents and teachers often make heroic efforts to find adequate help for their SLD children. The challenge for the future is clearly to put more efforts into devising and evaluating ways of overcoming or at least minimising the problems.

There is a sense that we are entering an era that has great potential for an improved outlook for children and families who have struggled with these difficulties. We know a great deal more than we used to, about children's learning, what helps, and what hinders. We should beware of unsubstantiated claims for treatments that have no sound theoretical or empirical basis, and try to evaluate the remedial methods we do choose, so that we know where to get best value for effort. Community and political awareness of learning difficulties in school-aged children is increasing, although we may argue that it needs to expand much more. The importance of early home and pre-school experience with language, ideas, books, counting, and creative activities is often publicised. With political will, backed up by the necessary resourcing, the knowledge we have gained can be expected to impact positively on our efforts to provide a better outcome for SLD children.

References

Aaron, P.G. (1982). The neuropsychology of developmental dyslexia. In R.N. Malatesha, & P.G. Aaron (Eds.), *Reading disorders: Varieties and treatments* (pp.5–67). New York: Academic Press.

Adams, M. J. (1990). *Beginning to read: Thinking and learning about print.* Cambridge, MA: MIT Press.

Anderson, V., Lajoie, G., & Bell, R. (1995). *Neuropsychological assessment of the school-aged child.* Department of Psychology, Melbourne University.

Ansara, A. (1982). The Orton-Gillingham approach to remediation in developmental dyslexia. In R.N. Malatesha, & P.G. Aaron (Eds.), *Reading disorders: Varieties and treatments* (pp.409–433). New York: Academic Press.

Ashcraft, M.H., Yamashita, T.S., & Aram, D.M. (1992). Mathematics performance in left and right brain-lesioned children. *Brain and Cognition, 19,* 208–252.

Badian, N.A. (1983). Dyscalculia and nonverbal disorders of learning. In H.R. Myklebust (Ed.), *Progress in learning disabilities.* (Vol. 5, pp.235–264). New York: Stratton.

Baker, L., & Cantwell, D.P. (1985). Developmental arithmetic disorder. In H.I. Kaplan, & B.J. Sadock (Eds.), *Comprehensive textbook of psychiatry.* (Vol. 2, 4th ed., pp.1697–1700). Baltimore: Williams & Wilkins.

Baydar, N., Brooks-Gunn, J., & Furstenberg, F.F. (1993). Early warning signs of functional illiteracy: Predictors in childhood and adolescence. *Child Development, 64,* 815–829.

Beck, I., & Juel, C. (1992). The role of decoding in learning to read. In S. J. Samuels & A. Farstrup (Eds.), *What research has to say about reading instruction* (pp.101–123). Newark, Delaware: International Reading Association.

Beery, K.E. (1967). *Developmental test of visual-motor integration. Administration and scoring manual*. Chicago: Follett Publishing.

Benton, A.L. (1974). *Revised visual retention test* (4th ed.). New York: The Psychological Corporation.

Benton, A.L. (1975). Developmental dyslexia: Neurological aspects. In W.J. Friedlander (Ed.), *Advances in neurology* (Vol. 7, pp.1–46). New York: Raven Press.

Berger, M., Yule, W., & Rutter, M. (1975). Attainment and adjustment in two geographical areas–II: The prevalence of specific reading retardation. *British Journal of Psychiatry, 126*, 510–519.

Boyd, T.A. (1988). Clinical assessment of memory in children: A developmental framework for practice. In M.G. Tramontana, & S.R. Hooper (Eds.), *Assessment issues in child neuropsychology* (pp.177–204). New York: Plenum Press.

Bradley, L. (1980). *Assessing reading difficulties*. London: Macmillan Educational.

Bradley, L. (1981). The organisation of motor patterns for spelling: An effective remedial strategy for backward readers. *Developmental Medicine and Child Neurology, 23*, 83–91.

Bradley, L. (1982). An experimental evaluation of effective remedial techniques for the learning disabled. *Thalamus, 2*(1), 43–59.

Bradley, L., & Bryant, P.E. (1983). Categorising sounds and learning to read: A causal connection. *Nature, 301*, 419.

Bryant P.E. (1995). Children and Arithmetic. *Journal of Child Psychology and Psychiatry, 36*(1), 3–32.

Bryant, P.E., & Bradley, L. (1980). Why children sometimes write words which they do not read. In U.Frith (Ed.), *Cognitive processes in spelling* (pp.355–372). London: Academic Press.

Bryant, P.E. & Bradley, L. (1985). *Children's reading problems*. Oxford: Blackwell.

Bryant, P.E., & Impey, L. (1986). The similarities between normal readers and developmental and acquired dyslexics. *Cognition, 24*, 121–137.

Bushke, H. (1974). Components of verbal learning in children: Analysis by selective reminding. *Journal of Experimental Child Psychology, 18*, 488–596.

Byrne, B., & Fielding-Barnsley, R. (1993). Evaluation of a program to teach phonemic awareness to young children: A 1–year follow-up. *Journal of Educational Psychology, 85*(1), 104–111.

Byrne, B., & Fielding-Barnsley, R. (1995). Evaluation of a program to teach phonemic awareness to young children: A 2– and 3–year follow-up, and a new preschool trial, *Journal of Educational Psychology, 87*, 488–503.

Byrne, B., Freebody, P., & Gates, A. (1992). Longitudinal data on the relations of word-reading strategies to comprehension, reading time, and phonemic awareness. *Reading Research Quarterly, 27*, 141–151.

Castles, A., & Coltheart, M. (1993). Varieties of developmental dyslexia. *Cognition, 47*, 149–180.

Ceci, S.J., & Peters, D.J. (1980). Dyscalculia and the perceptual deficit hypothesis: A correlational study. *Focus on Learning Problems in Mathematics, 2*(1), 11–14.

Center, Y., Wheldall, K., & Freeman, L. (1992). Evaluating the effectiveness of reading recovery: A critique. *Educational Psychology, 12*(3/4) , 263–274.

Clay, M.M. (1985). *The early detection of reading difficulties*. London: Heinmann.

Coltheart, M., & Rastle, K. (1994). Serial processing in reading aloud: Evidence for dual-route models of reading. *Journal of Experimental Psychology: Human Perception and Performance, 20*(6), 1197–1211.

Coltheart, M., Curtis, B., Atkins, P., & Haller, M. (1993). Models of reading aloud: Dual route and parallel distributed processing approaches. *Psychological Review, 100*, 589–605.

Coltheart, M., Masterson, J., Byng, S., Prior, M., & Riddoch, M.J. (1983). Surface dyslexia. *Quarterly Journal of Experimental Psychology, 37A*, 469–495.

Connolly, A. (1988). *Key math revised: A diagnostic inventory of essential mathematics*. Circle Pines, MN: American Guidance Services.

Cumming, G., Galante, V., & Prior, M. (1987). A speaking and feeling computer helps children learn to read. *Education Research and Perspectives, 14*(1), 24–38.

Daniels, J.C., & Diack, H. (1958). *The Standard Reading Tests*. London: Chatto & Windus Ltd.

Di Simoni, F. (1978). *The Token Test for children*. Highman, MA: Teaching Resources.

Elliot, C.D., Murray, D.J., & Pearson, L.S. (1983). *British Ability Scales* (2nd ed.). London: NFER-Nelson Publishing Company.

Ellis, A.W. (1984). *Reading, writing and dyslexia*. Hove, UK: Lawrence Erlbaum Associates Ltd.

Ellis, A.W. & Young, A. (1988). *Human cognitive neuropsychology*. Hove, UK: Lawrence Erlbaum Associates Ltd.

Engelmann, S. & Bruner, E.C. (1969). *Distar reading I and II: An instructional system*. Chicago: Science Research Associates.

Evans, J.R. (1982). Neuropsychologically based remedial reading procedures: Some possibilities. In R.N. Malatesha & P.G. Aaron (Eds.), *Reading disorders: Varieties and treatments* (pp.371–388). New York: Academic Press.

Farnham-Diggory, S. (1978). *Learning disabilities: The developing child*. London: Fontana/Open Books.

Fawcett, A.J., Nicolson, R.I., & Morris, S. (1993). Computer-based spelling remediation for dyslexic children. *Journal of Computer Assisted Learning, 9*, 171–183.

Fergusson, D.M., & Horwood, L.J. (1995). Predictive validity of categorically and dimensionally scored measures of disruptive childhood behaviors. *Journal of Child Psychology and Psychiatry, 34*(4), 477–488.

Fletcher, J.M., & Loveland, K.A. (1986). Neuropsychology of arithmetic disabilities in children. *Focus on Learning Problems in Mathematics, 8*(2), 23–40.

Forehand, R., & Long, N. (1988). Outpatient treatment of the acting out child: Procedures, long term follow-up data, and clinical problems, *Advances in Behaviour Research and Therapy, 10*, 129–177.

Forrester, G., & Geffen, G.M. (1991). Performance measures of 7 to 15 year old children on the Auditory Verbal Learning Test. *The Clinical Neuropsychologist, 5*, 345–359.

Frick, P.J., Kamphaus, R.W., Lahey, B.B., Loeber, R., Christ, M.A.G., Hart, E.L., & Tannembaum, L.E. (1991). Academic underachievement and the disruptive behaviour disorders. *Journal of Consulting and Clinical Psychology, 59*, 289–294.

Frith, U. (1978). Annotation: Spelling difficulties. *Journal of Child Psychology and Psychiatry, 19*, 279–218.

Frith, U. (1980). Unexpected spelling problems. In U. Frith (Ed.), *Cognitive processes in spelling* (pp.495–516). London: Academic Press.

Frith, U. (1985). Beneath the surface of developmental dyslexia. In K. E. Patterson, J. C. Marshall, & M. Coltheart (Eds.), *Surface dyslexia*. Hove, UK: Lawrence Erlbaum Associates Ltd.

Fuson, K.C. (1984). More complexities in subtraction. *Journal for Research in Mathematics Education; 15*(3), 214–225.

Fuson, K.C. (1986). Roles of representation of verbalization in the teaching of multi-digit addition and subtraction Special Issue: Psychology and the learning of mathematics. *European Journal of Psychology of Education; 1*(2), 35–56.

Fuson, K.C. (1988). *Children's counting and concepts of number*. New York: Springer-Verlag.

Garnett, K., & Fleischner, J.E. (1987). Mathematical disabilities. *Pediatric Annals, 16*(2), 159–176.

Garzia, R. (1993). Optometric factors in reading disabilities. In D.M. Willows, R.S. Kruk, & E. Corcos (Eds.), *Visual processes in reading and reading disabilities.* (pp.419–434). Hillsdale, NJ: Lawrence Erlbaum Associates Inc.

Geary, D.C. (1993). Mathematical disabilities: Cognitive, neuropsychological, and genetic components. *Psychological Bulletin, 114*(2), 345–362.

Gentry, R. (1987). *Spel...is a four-letter word*. Ontario, Canada: Scholastic.

Gillingham, A., & Stillman, B. (1979). *Remedial training for children with specific disabilities in reading and penmanship*. Cambridge, MA: Educators Publishing Service.

Ginsburg, H. (1977). *Children's arithmetic: The learning process*. New York: Van Nostrand.

Gittelman, R., & Feingold, I. (1983). Children with reading disorders-I. Efficacy of reading remediation. *Journal of Child Psychology and Psychiatry, 24*(2), 167–191.

Glynn, T., Fairweather, R., & Donald, S. (1992). Involving parents in improving children's learning at school: Policy issues for behavioural research. *Behaviour Change, 9*(3), 178–185.

Glynn, T., McNaughton, S., Robinson, V., & Quinn, M. (1979). *Remedial reading at home: Helping you to help your child*. Wellington: New Zealand Council for Educational Research.

Goswami, U., & Bryant, P. (1990). *Phonological skills and learning to read*. Hove, UK: Lawrence Erlbaum Associates Ltd.

Grafman, J., Kampen, D., Rosenberg, J., Salazar, A. et al. (1989). Calculation abilities in a patient with a virtual left hemispherectomy. *Behavioural Neurology, 2*(3), 183–194.

Gredler, G. (1990). Approaches to the remediation of learning difficulties. In R.M. Gupta & P. Coxhead (Eds.), *Intervention with children*. (pp.171–198). London: Routledge.

Gredler, G. (1992). *School readiness: Assessment and educational issues*. Brandon, VT: Clinical Psychology Publishing Company.

Gronwall, D.M.A., & Sampson, H. (1974). *The psychological effects of concussion*. Auckland, NZ: Auckland University Press.

Hatcher, P.J., Hulme, C., & Ellis, A.W. (1994). Ameliorating early reading failure by integrating the teaching of reading and phonological skills: The phonological linkage hypothesis. *Child Development, 65*, 41–57.

Hecaen, H. (1976). Acquired aphasia in children and the ontogenesis of hemispheric functional specialization. *Brain and Language, 3*, 114–134.

Hewison, J. (1988). The long term effectiveness of parental involvement in reading: A follow-up to the Haringey Reading Project. *British Journal of Educational Psychology, 58*, 184–190.

Hinshaw, S.P. (1992). Externalizing behavior problems and academic underachievement in childhood and adolescence: Causal relationships and underlying mechanisms. *Psychological Bulletin, 111*(1), 127–155.

Hinshelwood, J. (1895). Word-blindness and visual memory. *Lancet, 2*, 1564–1570.

Hooper, S.R., & Willis, W.G. (1989). *Learning disability subtyping: Neuropsychological foundations, conceptual models, and issues in clinical differentiation*. New York: Springer Verlag.

Hornsby, B., & Miles, T.R. (1980). The effects of a dyslexia-centred teaching programme. *British Journal of Educational Psychology, 50*, 236–242.

Hornsby, B., & Shear, F. (1978). *Alpha to omega: The A–Z of teaching, reading, writing & spelling* (2nd ed.). London: Heinemann Educational Books.

Hughes, M. (1986). *Children and number: Difficulties in learning mathematics*. Oxford: Blackwell.

Hulme, C. (1981). *Reading retardation and multi-sensory teaching*. London: Routledge & Kegan Paul.

Iversen, A.J., & Tunmer, W.E. (1993). Phonological processing skills and the reading recovery program. *Journal of Educational Psychology, 85*, 112–126.

Johnson, D.D. (1974). Sex differences in reading across cultures. *Reading Research Quarterly, 1*, 67–86.

Jorm, A.F. (1983). *The psychology of reading and spelling disabilities*. London: Routledge & Kegan Paul.

Kavale, K.A. (1988). Epistemological relativity in learning disabilities. *Journal of Learning Disabilities, 21*, 215–218.

Kazdin, A.E. (1987). Treatment of antisocial behavior in children: Current status and future directions. *Psychological Bulletin, 102*, 187–203.

Kirk, S.A., McCarthy, J.J., & Kirk, W.D. (1968). *The Illinois Test of Psycholinguistic Abilities* (rev. ed.). Urbana: University of Illinois Press.

Kline, C.L., & Kline, C.L. (1975). Follow up study of 216 dyslexic children. *Bulletin of the Orton Society, 25*, 127–144.

Lewis, C., Hitch, G.J., & Walker, P. (1994). The prevalence of specific arithmetic difficulties and specific reading difficulties in 9- to 10-year-old boys and girls. *Journal of Child Psychology and Psychiatry, 35*(2), 283–292.

Limbrick, L., McNaughton, S., & Cameron, M. (1985). Peer tutoring. *Set, Research Information For Teachers, 12*(2), 1–4.

Links, P.S., Boyle, M.H., & Offord, D.R. (1989). The prevalence of emotional disorder in children. *Journal of Nervous and Mental Disease, 177*, 85–91.

Long, P., Forehand, R., Wierson, M., & Morgan, A. (1994). Does parent training with young noncompliant children have long-term effects? *Behavior Research and Therapy, 32*, 101–107.

Lovett, M.W., Benson, N.J., & Olds, J. (1990). Individual difference predictors of treatment outcome in the remediation of specific reading disability. *Learning and Individual Differences, 2*(3), 287–314.

Lovett, M.W., Borden, S.L., DeLuca, T., Lacrerenza, L., Benson, N.J., & Brackstone, D. (1994). Treating the core deficits of developmental dyslexia: Evidence of transfer of learning after phonologically- and strategy-based reading training programs. *Developmental Psychology, 30*, 805–822.

Lundberg, I., Frost, J., & Petersen, O. (1988). Effects of an extensive program for stimulating phonological awareness in preschool children. *Reading Research Quarterly, 23*, 263–284.

Luria, A.R. (1966). *Human brain and psychological processes*. New York: Harper & Row.

Luria, A.R. (1970). *Traumatic aphasia: Its syndromes, psychology and treatment*. The Hague: Mouton.

Luria, A.R. (1980). *Higher cortical functions in man*. (2nd ed.). New York: Basic Books.

Lyon, G., Moats, L., & Flynn, J. (1988). From assessment to treatment: Linkage to interventions with children. In M. Tramontana & S. Hooper (Eds.), *Assessment issues in child neuropsychology* (pp.113–144). New York: Plenum Press.

Mann, V.A., & Brady, S. (1988). Reading disability: The role of language deficiencies. *Journal of Consulting and Clinical Psychology, 56*(6), 811–816.

Marsh, G., Friedman, M., Welch, V., & Desberg, P. (1981). A cognitive-developmental theory of reading acquisition. In G. Mackinnon & T. Waller (Eds.), *Reading research: Advances in theory and practice* (Vol. 3, pp.142–176). New York : Academic Press.

Mastropieri, M.A., Scruggs, T.E., & Shiah, S. (1991). Mathematics instruction for learning disabled students: A review of research. *Learning Disabilities: Research and Practice, 6*(2), 89–98.

Maughan, B. (1995). Annotation: Long-term outcomes of developmental reading problems. *Journal of Psychology and Psychiatry, 36*(3), 357–371.

Maughan, B., Hagell, A., Rutter, M., & Yule, W. (1994). Poor readers in secondary school. *Reading and Writing: An Interdisciplinary Journal, 6*, 125–150.

McCloskey, M. (1992). Cognitive mechanisms in numerical processing: Evidence from acquired dyscalculia. *Cognition, 44*, 107–157.

McCorriston, M.E. (1991). *Cognitive processing strategies and sublexical orthographic knowledge in developmental dysgraphia*. Unpublished PhD thesis, La Trobe University, Bundoora.

McCorriston, M.E., & McKenzie, B.E. (1981). The role of morphological knowledge in spelling difficulties. In A.R. Nesdale, C. Pratt, R. Grieve, J. Field, D. Illingworth, & J. Hogben (Eds.). *Advances in child development: Theory and research* (pp.94–100). University of Western Australia.

McGee, R., & Feehan, M. (1991). Are girls with problems of attention underrecognized? *Journal of Psychopathology and Behavioral Assessment, 13*(3), 187–198.

McGee, R., Williams, S., Share, D.L., Anderson, J. & Silva, P.A. (1986). The relationship between specific reading retardation, general reading backwardness and behavioural problems in a large sample of Dunedin boys: A longitudinal study from five to eleven years. *Journal of Child Psychology and Psychiatry and Allied Disciplines, 27*(5), 597–610.

Morgan, R. & Ryan, E. (1979). "Paired Reading." A preliminary report on a technique for parental tuition of reading retarded children. *Journal of Child Psychology and Psychiatry, 20*, 151–160.

Morris, G., Levy, J., & Pirozzolo, F. (1988). Electrophysiological assessment in learning disabilities. In M. Tramontana & S. Hooper (Eds.), *Assessment issues in child neuropsychology* (pp.337–368). New York: Plenum Press.

Moyer, S. B. (1979). Rehabilitation of alexia: A case study. *Cortex, 15*, 139–144.

Munro, J. (1986). The mathematics underachiever as a passive learner. *Success in Learning Mathematics, 1*(3), 2–14.

Murray, P.L., & Mayer, R.E. (1988). Preschool children's judgements of number magnitude. *Journal of Educational Psychology, 80*(2), 206–109.

Neale, M.D. (1988). *Neale analysis of reading ability – Revised.* Hawthorn: Australian Council for Educational Research.

Nelson, N.E., & Warrington, E.K. (1974). Developmental spelling retardation and its relation to other cognitive abilities. *British Journal of Psychology, 65*, 265–274.

O'Hare, A.E., Brown, J.K., & Aitken, K. (1991). Dyscalculia in children. *Developmental Medicine and Child Neurology, 33*, 356–361.

Olson, R.K., & Wise, B.W. (1992). Reading on the computer with orthographic and speech feedback: An overview of the Colorado remediation project. *Reading and Writing: An Interdisciplinary Journal, 4*, 107–144.

Olson, R.K., Wise, B.W., Conners, F., Rack, J.P., & Fulker, D. (1989). Specific deficits in component reading and language skills: Genetic and environmental influences. *Journal of Learning Disabilities, 22*, 339–348.

Orton, S.T. (1925). Word-blindness in school children. *Archives of Neurology and Psychiatry, 14*, 582–615.

Orton, S.T. (1937). *Reading, writing, and speech problems in children.* New York: Norton.

Prior, M. (1989). Reading disability: "Normative" or "pathological". *Australian Journal of Psychology, 41*(2), 135–158.

Prior, M., Frye, S., & Fletcher, C. (1987). Remediation for subgroups of retarded readers using a modified oral spelling procedure. *Developmental Medicine and Child Neurology, 29*, 64–71.

Prior, M., & McCorriston, M. (1985). Surface dyslexia: A regression effect? *Brain and Language, 25*(1), 52–71

Prior, M., Sanson, A.V., Smart, D.F., & Oberklaid, F. (1995). Reading disability in an Australian community sample. *Australian Journal of Psychology, 47*(1), 32–37.

Prior, M., Smart, D.F., Sanson, A.V., & Oberklaid, F. (1993). Sex differences in psychological adjustment from infancy to eight years. *Journal of the American Academy of Child and Adolescent Psychiatry, 32*, 291–304.

Rack, J.P., Snowling, M.J., & Olson, R.K. (1992). The nonword reading deficit in developmental dyslexia: A review. *Reading Research Quarterly, 27*(1), 29–53.

Read, C. (1986). *Children's creative spelling.* London: Routledge & Kegan Paul.

Reid, J.B. (1993). Prevention of conduct disorder before and after school entry: Relating interventions to developmental findings. *Development and Psychopathology, 5*, 243–262.

Rourke, B.P., & Del Dotto, J. (1994). *Learning disabilities: A neuro-psychological perspective.* Thousand Oaks, CA: Sage Publications.

Rourke, B.P., & Tsatsanis, K.D. (1995). Memory disturbances of children with learning disabilities: A neuropsychological analysis of two academic achievement subtypes. In A. Baddeley, B. Wilson, & F. Watts (Eds.), *Handbook of memory disorders.* Chichester, UK: John Wiley.

Rutter, M., & Giller, H. (1983). *Juvenile delinquency: Trends and perspectives.* New York: Penguin Books.

Rutter, M., & Yule, W. (1975). The concept of specific reading retardation. *Journal of Child Psychology and Psychiatry, 16*, 181–197.

Sanders, M.R. (Ed.) (1995). *Healthy families, healthy nation: Strategies for promoting family mental health in Australia*. Brisbane: Australian Academic Press.

Sanders, M.R., & Dadds, M.R. (1993). *Behavioural family intervention*. Needham Heights, MA: Allyn & Bacon.

Sanson, A.V. (1984). *Sub-classification of hyperactive children*. Unpublished PhD thesis, La Trobe University, Bundoora.

Sattler, J.M. (1992). *Assessment of children*. (3rd ed.). San Diego: J.M. Sattler.

Scruggs, T.E., & Wong, B.Y.L. (1990). *Intervention research in learning disabilities*. New York: Springer-Verlag.

Seymour, P.H.K., & Bunce, F. (1992). Application of cognitive models to remediation in cases of developmental dyslexia. In M.J. Riddoch & G.W. Humphreys (Eds.), *Cognitive neuropsychology and cognitive rehabilitation* (pp.349–377). Hove, UK: Lawrence Erlbaum Associates Ltd.

Shalev, R.S., Auerbach, J., & Gross-Tur, V., (1995) Developmental dyscalculia behavioural and attentional aspects: A research note. *Journal of Child psychology and Psychiatry, 36*(7), 1261– 1268.

Shankweiler, D., Crain, S., Katz, L., Fowler, A.E., Liberman, A.M., Brady, S.A., Thornton, R., Lundquist, E., Dreyer, L., Fetcher, J.M., Stuebing, K.K., Shaywitz, S.E., & Shaywitz, B.A. (1995). Cognitive profiles of reading-disabled children: Comparison of language skills in phonology, morphology, and syntax. *Psychological Science, 6*(3), 149–156.

Share, D.L. (1995). Phonological recoding and self-teaching: Sine qua non of reading acquisition. *Cognition, 55*, 151–218.

Share, D.L., Moffitt, T.E., & Silva, P.A. (1988). Factors associated with arithmetic-and-reading disability and specific arithmetic disability. *Journal of Learning Disabilities, 21*(5), 313–320.

Shaywitz, S.E., Escobar, M.D., Shaywitz, B.A., Fletcher, J.M., & Makuch, R. (1992). Evidence that dyslexia may represent the lower tail of a normal distribution of reading ability. *The New England Journal of Medicine, 326,*(3), 145–150.

Shaywitz, S.E., Shaywitz, B.A., Fletcher, J.M., & Escobar, M.D. (1990). Prevalence of reading disability in boys and girls: Results of the Connecticut Longitudinal Study. *Journal of the American Medical Association, 264*(8), 998–1002.

Sheslow, D., & Adams, W. (1990). *Wide Range Assessment of Memory and Learning (WRAML)*. Delaware: Wide Range.

Siegel, L.S. (1985). Psycholinguistic aspects of reading disabilities. In L.S. Siegel, & F.J. Morrison (Eds.), *Cognitive development in atypical children* (pp.45–66). New York: Springer-Verlag.

Siegel, L.S. (1989). IQ is irrelevant to the definition of learning disabilities. *Journal of Learning Disabilities, 22*, 469–478, 486.

Siegel, L.S., & Linder, B.A. (1984). Short-term memory processes in children with reading and arithmetic learning disabilities. *Developmental Psychology, 20*(2), 200–207.

Siegel, L.S., & Ryan, E.B. (1988). Development of grammatical sensitivity, phonological, and short-term memory skills in normally achieving and learning disabled children. *Developmental Psychology, 24*, 28–37.

Snowling, M. (1987). *Dyslexia. A cognitive developmental perspective*. Oxford: Blackwell.

Snowling, M.J. (1991). Developmental reading disorders. *Journal of Child Psychology and Psychiatry and Allied Disciplines, 32*(1), 49–77.

Spreen, O. (1988). Prognosis of learning disability. *Journal of Consulting and Clinical Psychology, 56*(6), 836–842.

Spreen O., & Strauss, E. (1991). *A compendium of neuropsychological tests.* New York: Oxford University Press.

Stanovich, K.E. (1986). Matthew effects in reading: Some consequences of individual differences in the acquisition of literacy. *Reading Research Quarterly, 21*(4), 360–406.

Stanovich, K.E. (1994). Does dyslexia exist? *Journal of Child Psychology and Psychiatry, 35,* 579–596.

Stevenson, H.W., Stigler, J.W., Lucker, G.W., & Lee, S. (1982). Reading disabilities: The case of Chinese, Japanese, and English. *Child Development, 53,* 1164–1181.

Stevenson, J. (1991). Which aspects of processing text mediate genetic effects? *Reading and Writing: An Interdisciplinary Journal, 3,* 249–269.

Stevenson, J., Graham, P., Fredman, G., & McLoughlin, V. (1987). A twin study of genetic influences on reading and spelling ability and disability. *Journal of Child Psychology and Psychiatry, 28,* 229–247.

Strang, J.D., & Rourke, B.P. (1985). Arithmetic disability subtypes: The neuropsychological significance of specific arithmetical impairment in childhood. In B.P. Rourke (Ed.), *Neuropsychology of learning disabilities: Essentials of subtype analysis* (pp.167–183). New York: Guilford Press.

Swanson, H.L. (1993). Working memory in learning disability subgroups: *Journal of Experimental Child Psychology, 56*(1), 87–114.

Swanson, H.L. (1994). Short-term memory and working memory: Do both contribute to our understanding of academic achievement in children and adults with learning disabilities? *Journal of Learning Disabilities, 27*(1), 34–50.

Taylor, H.G., Fletcher, J.M., & Satz, P. (1982).Component processes in reading disabilities: Neuropsychological investigation of distinct reading subskill deficits. In R.N. Malatesha & P.G. Aaron (Eds.), *Reading disorders: Varieties and treatments* (pp.121–147). New York: Academic Press.

Temple, C. (1991). Procedural dyscalculia and number fact dyscalculia: Double dissociation in developmental dyscalculia. *Cognitive Neuropsychology, 8,* 155–176.

Thompson, L.A., Detterman, D.K., & Plomin, R. (1991). Associations between cognitive abilities and scholastic achievement: Genetic overlap and environmental differences. *Psychological Science, 2,* 158–165.

Tramontana, M.G., & Hooper, S.R. (Eds.). (1988). *Assessment issues in child neuropsychology.* New York: Plenum Press.

Vellutino, F.R. (1978). Toward an understanding of dyslexia: Psychological factors in specific reading disability. In A. L. Benton, & D. Pearl (Eds.), *Dyslexia: An appraisal of current knowledge* (pp.61–111). New York: Oxford University Press.

Vellutino, F.R. (1979). *Dyslexia: Theory and research.* Cambridge, MA: MIT Press.

Vellutino, F.R. (1991). Has basic research in reading increased our understanding of developmental reading and how to teach reading? *Psychological Science, 70*(2), 81–83.

Vellutino, F.R., Scanlon, D.M., & Tanzman, M.S. (1991). Bridging the gap between cognitive and neuropsychological conceptualizations of reading disability. *Learning and Individual Differences, 3*, 181–203.

Vogel, S.A. (1990). Gender differences in intelligence, language, visual-motor abilities and academic achievement in students with learning disabilities: A review of the literature. *Journal of Learning Difficulties, 23*, 44–52.

Wagner, R.K., Torgesen, J.K., & Rashotte, C.A. (1994). Development of reading-related phonological processing abilities: New evidence of bi-directional causality from a latent variable longitudinal study. *Developmental Psychology, 30*(1), 73–87.

Webster-Stratton, C., & Herbert, M. (1994). *Troubled families—Problem children. Working with parents: A collaborative process.* Chichester, UK: John Wiley & Sons.

Wilkening, G.N. (1984). The neuropsychologic assessment of arithmetic disorders in children. *Focus on Learning Problems in Mathematics, 6*(4), 59–76.

Williams, S., & McGee, R. (1994). Reading attainment and juvenile delinquency. *Journal of Child Psychology and Psychiatry and Allied Disciplines, 35*(3), 441–459.

Willows, D.M., Kruk, R.S., & Corcos E. (Eds.). (1993). *Visual processes in reading and reading disabilities.* Hillsdale, NJ: Lawrence Erlbaum Associates Inc.

Wise B.W., & Olson, R.K. (1995). Computer-based phonological awareness and reading instruction. *Annals of Dyslexia, 45*, 99–122.

Wong, B., Harris, K., & Graham. S. (1991) Academic applications of cognitive-behavioral programs with learning disabled students. In P.C. Kendall (Ed.), *Child and adolescent therapy: Cognitive behavioural responses* (pp.245–275). New York: Guilford Press.

Author index

177

Subject index